OXFORD
LATIN
COURSE

TEACHER'S BOOK
PART I
SECOND EDITION

CONTENTS

MAURICE BALME & JAMES MORWOOD

OXFORD
UNIVERSITY PRESS

OXFORD

UNIVERSITY PRESS

Great Clarendon Street, Oxford OX2 6DP

Oxford University Press is a department of the University of Oxford.
It furthers the University's objective of excellence in research,
scholarship, and education by publishing worldwide in

Oxford New York

Athens Auckland Bangkok Bogotá Buenos Aires Cape Town
Chennai Dar es Salaam Delhi Florence Hong Kong Istanbul
Karachi Kolkata Kuala Lumpur Madrid Melbourne Mexico City
Mumbai Nairobi Paris São Paulo Shanghai Singapore Taipei
Tokyo Toronto Warsaw

with associated companies in Berlin Ibadan

Oxford is a registered trade mark of Oxford University Press
in the UK and in certain other countries

© Oxford University Press 1996

Reprinted 1997, 1999, 2000, 2001

ISBN 0 19 912230 X

Typeset and designed by Positif Press, Oxford
Printed and bound in Great Britain by
Butler & Tanner Ltd, Frome and London

Introduction

We have made this revision of the Oxford Latin Course in response to many suggestions received from teachers in both Britain and the United States; we are extremely grateful for their encouraging and constructive response to our queries. While the basic principles of the course remain the same, we have introduced several changes.

What is different about the New Oxford Latin Course?

The biggest change we have made is to split the course into four parts instead of three. Part I uses only the present tense of the verb together with imperatives, present infinitive and the first three declensions. Part II completes the indicative tenses of the verb, active and passive, and introduces the 4th and 5th declensions. Part III immediately introduces the subjunctive and covers all common Latin syntax; it is inevitably longer than the first two parts and incorporates a fair amount of 'real' Latin in the later chapters. The final part is a straight reader of the same authors as those presented in the old Part III.

We have reduced the length of some of the stories. In a reading course that relies partly on an inductive method, it is essential that students should read as much continuous Latin as possible. However, a reading course must reflect the fact that the time allowed for teaching Latin has now been cut to the bone.

In order to reflect a wider cross-section of Roman society we have given female figures a greater role in the course, for instance by sending Horatia to school with Quintus and by including the stories of Psyche and Cloelia (Part I) and by adding letters from Scintilla to Flaccus and Quintus (Part II). We have likewise increased the amount of narrative that deals with daily life.

The learning curve of grammar and syntax has been made more gentle. In all parts there are several chapters in which little or no new grammar is introduced, to give students a chance to catch their breath.

Another big change is that each book is now divided in two; the narratives, comprehension exercises and background essays come first; then, in the second half of each book, come the grammatical explanations and exercises. This has two advantages: first, the narratives present an uninterrupted story with social and historical comment in the essays; second, the presentation of the grammar is made clearer.

We have expanded the grammatical explanations to some extent, filling in some gaps (e.g. the vocative and the mixed conjugation are explained in their proper places). The fuller grammatical explanations may afford some difficulty to younger students; we suggest that teachers handle these as suits the age and ability of their students, perhaps by using less grammatical terminology.

We have added four new types of exercise: (1) the occasional short playlet, to encourage students to speak Latin aloud fluently and expressively; (2) Respondē Latīnē exercises, in which students are asked to answer questions on the narrative in Latin; (3) grammatical exercises concentrating on the different parts of the verb; (4) word-building exercises intended to increase students' vocabulary.

Much of the background material has been completely rewritten, partly in order to cover hitherto neglected aspects of the ancient world. We have also considerably increased the amount of primary source material in the essays, so that students may be encouraged to make a direct response to the activities and attitudes of the ancient world.

We have added an appendix to each part, which gives a longer passage of continuous Latin to encourage fluent reading.

The Teacher's Book now includes an expanded commentary on points of language and background, translations of all narratives and exercises, as well as three attainment tests.

The aims of the course

Our aims throughout the course have been for the student:
1   to develop, at an appropriate level, a competence in the language studied;
2   to read, understand, appreciate and make a personal response to some of the literature in the original language;
3   to acquire some understanding of the civilization within which the literature studied was produced;
4   to develop a sensitive and an analytical approach to language by seeing English in relation to a language of very different structure and by observing the influence of the ancient language on our own;
5   to develop the ability to observe, abstract and analyse information, paying due regard to evidence, and to develop a sympathetic awareness of others' motives and attitudes.

These admirable but ambitious aims match those of the GCSE National Criteria for Classical subjects in the UK. They are unlikely to be achieved unless, from the very start, our students read Latin not as a linguistic jigsaw but as a vehicle for conveying meaning to which they habitually make a personal response. We have tried to construct a narrative that will evoke such a response, at first at a simple level, but gradually becoming more sophisticated. As students develop some understanding of Roman culture and history through the Latin narrative, the illustrations and the background sections that conclude each chapter, and as Horace himself slowly emerges as a sympathetic character, they may respond intelligently to the actual poems embedded in the later stages of the narrative.

The structure of the course

Of the four parts into which the course is now divided, the first three provide an introduction to the language, culture and literature of the Romans. By the end of Part III basic grammar and syntax have been covered and the student should be ready to tackle unabridged texts. The final part is a reader, containing passages from Golden Age authors – Caesar, Cicero, Catullus, Virgil, Livy and Ovid.

The first three parts take the form of a narrative which tells the story of the life of the poet Horace. Part I covers his boyhood and schooling in Venusia, with digressions when his schoolmaster tells stories from the *Iliad* and *Aeneid*, to which are now added stories told by Scintilla and Flaccus to their children. In Part II Flaccus takes Horace to Rome to the school of Orbilius. He goes on to study under the rhetor Heliodorus and then proceeds to the Academy in Athens. This part ends with the murder of Cicero, the father of Quintus' friend Marcus. In Part III, with the arrival of Brutus in Athens, Quintus becomes involved in political events and joins the army of Brutus. After the defeat and death of Brutus, he returns to Italy; his parents have disappeared in the chaos of civil war, and he goes to Rome. We then trace his career as a poet and his friendship with Virgil, Maecenas and Augustus. Part III ends with the deaths of Maecenas and Horace himself.

Part I is fictional, its fictions adhering to the few facts we know. Part II, though containing a great deal of fiction, is structured round known facts. Part III sees Horace at the centre of world-shaking events and moves much closer to history; in this part we often quote from contemporary authors, including a fair amount of Horace's own poetry.

It is impossible to make sensible recommendations on how long to spend on each part, as there are so many variants – the number of periods allowed each week, the ability and age of the students, whether students have studied any other foreign language, etc. If the time factor means

that any of the course must be omitted, we suggest that the fabellae are the least important features in respect of narrative coherence and it is probably they that should be sacrificed.

Why Horace?

The choice of Horace as the central character has several advantages. First, his life covers the end of the republic and the Augustan revolution, the period of the Golden Age of Latin literature, which is the reading target at which we aim; and since Horace was involved in these great events, students acquire some understanding of the historical background to this literature. Second, Horace was an exact contemporary of the younger Marcus Cicero, to whom, at the cost of some bare-faced fiction, we give a major role in the story; this enables us to introduce his famous father, the one man about whom we know at first hand even more than we know about Horace himself. Third, his friendship with Virgil enables us to prepare the way for the extracts from the *Aeneid* that appear in the final part. By the time students come to read extracts from Caesar, Cicero and Virgil, the authors will be old friends, or at least acquaintances, whose social and historical background is already familiar. The literature will not, we hope, seem remote and unreal but related to what they have already read and relevant to their own experience.

Lastly, Horace's stay at university in Athens enables us to sketch in some of the Greek background to Roman literature; without some knowledge of this Roman poetry simply does not make sense, for, as Horace himself says:

Graecia capta ferum victōrem cēpit et artēs intulit agrestī Latiō.

Greece captured took its wild conqueror captive and brought the arts to rustic Latium.

(*Epistles* 2.1.155–6)

And so we intend that everything in the course should contribute to the overriding aim of preparing students to read the literature of the Golden Age with sympathetic understanding and intelligent appreciation.

Linguistic principles

We have tried to combine the best features of the modern and the traditional methods of teaching Latin. From the modern method, as exemplified by the Cambridge Latin Course, we accept that the aim of any Latin course should be the acquisition of reading skill and that everything else, linguistically speaking, should be subordinate to this aim. Hence translation from English into Latin is used only as an adjunct, to practise grammatical forms and concepts; for this purpose, we believe it has an important role in the early stages.

Second, we accept that the Latin language should be taught in a Roman context, so that understanding of the language and the culture proceed *pari passu*.

Third, we accept that the acquisition of reading skill is in part an inductive process; that is to say, the student learns from experiencing the language as an instrument conveying meaning, not simply by analysis. As a broad principle we believe that students should first read with understanding (and, if required, translate) and then study the grammar and syntax they have already met in context. We do not insist on a rigid application of this principle; if experience suggests that in some cases it is more helpful to do so, teachers may want to explain the grammar before reading the narrative. But it remains true that the first experience of new grammar and syntax always occurs before explanation, in the captions below the cartoons which introduce each chapter. Moreover, we believe that in fact students can, after understanding the cartoon captions, in nearly every chapter, go straight on to the narrative and read it with understanding.

Although we accept what we have called an 'inductive' approach, we also believe firmly in the necessity of learning vocabulary and grammar thoroughly. We do not hold that 'immersion' in the language will enable students to form a 'personal grammar', as we do in our native language. We tabulate all grammar in the traditional form, though the order in which we introduce it is not traditional.

We are well aware that for those brought up on the traditional method our approach may at times seem unsound, if not bizarre. It certainly takes courage for a teacher who has never tried it to plunge into this method of teaching the language. We can only say that it works in an extraordinary way and that it is much more entertaining for both teacher and taught than the traditional method; it results in quicker progress and holds the students' interest. Finally, if the grammar is properly learnt after the narrative is completed and the exercises are carefully done, the student will acquire as sound a grasp of the language as those brought up on a purely analytic approach and will eventually read Latin literature with more fluency and appreciation.

Teaching methods

Cartoon captions

Every chapter begins with cartoons, the captions of which introduce new linguistic points. Their meaning is intended to be self-evident and students should be able to read and understand them straight off with the help of the pictures. We suggest that you read them to your students and then ask them to read them aloud, paying attention to correct pronunciation. Understanding can then be tested either by question and answer in English or by translation.

After reading and understanding the captions, most students will be able to tackle the narrative with no further explanation until they come to study the grammar; they will in fact have have acquired an understanding of the new linguistic points inductively. In the text we do occasionally make explicit comment on new features. Teachers must judge whether more formal explanation is necessary before tackling the narrative but we do not on the whole consider it desirable. If students ask questions about the grammar you must answer them honestly, but with as little delay as possible.

Chapter vocabularies

We have put the chapter vocabularies before the narrative. We do not recommend that students should learn these vocabularies until after the narrative has been read (vocabulary sticks better if it has been encountered in a context), but their reading will be more fluent if they have first glanced through the lists of new words. We have kept these lists as short as possible in relation to our target; learning becomes easier as more words appear which are related to words already known.

We arrange the words under the headings: verbs, nouns, pronouns, adjectives, adverbs, prepositions, conjunctions. Students who are unfamiliar with the names of parts of speech will need some help with these terms, but teachers should not make too much of this. Students will soon come to understand them from experience.

Verbs are arranged alphabetically by conjugation – 1st, 2nd, 3rd, 4th, mixed;* nouns and adjectives by declensions – 1st, 2nd, 3rd, etc.

Immediately after the vocabularies we sometimes ask questions about English derivatives from Latin words in the vocabulary. This is intended both to help the meaning of the Latin words to stick and to increase the students' English vocabulary.

Glosses

Unknown words that do not appear in the vocabularies are glossed in the margin of the narrative passages and elsewhere, but when a word has appeared three times glossed, we cease to gloss it (e.g. **ecce!**, **valdē**). Some words, the meaning of which is clear from the context and English derivatives (e.g. **flamma** in a fire context), are intentionally omitted; their meaning must be 'guessed'. Such words do appear in the General vocabulary but we consider that such 'guessing' is an essential skill; students should not allow themselves to be held up by ignorance of a single word, the meaning of which is clear from the context.

* 1st, 2nd, 3rd, 3rd **-io**, 4th (US)

In the first few chapters students will be pleasantly surprised to find that they can read and understand an unknown and ancient language with such facility. When the first chapters are completed, they will be led on by the story, wanting to know what happens next and anticipating the meaning as we do in reading a book in our native language. For this reason most students will be prepared to pass over difficulties which are glossed but unexplained, so that, as we repeatedly say in the commentary, teachers need not be delayed by these difficulties; the essential grammar at any given stage is learnt chapter by chapter after reading the narrative.

Narrative passages

It is intended that the narratives should be treated orally and taken as fast as the ability of your students allows. If they are taken too slowly, boredom will result; if they are taken fast, fluency of understanding will follow. A foreign language should be learnt through the ear as well as through the eye. The narratives – indeed, all the Latin in the course – should be read aloud by the teacher and, as far as possible, also by students, before any translation is attempted; and it should be read fluently and expressively with correct pronunciation. Although this recommendation may seem time-consuming, the practice will in fact speed up progress and encourage fluent understanding, and it will discourage word-for-word silent translation, which is death to any appreciation of literature. Teachers may wish to tell their students that Latin writers designed their works to be read at recitals to audiences and so Latin literature cannot be fully appreciated unless it is read aloud. (A guide to pronunciation is included in the Students' Book (pp. 6–7), and practice in correct pronunciation, especially of vowels and diphthongs, should be the first thing to be taught.)

We want our students ultimately to understand Latin in Latin without translating. Although translation is the quickest and easiest method of testing understanding, teachers should not always require translation of the whole of every narrative, but should sometimes ask comprehension questions on a paragraph as a variant method of testing. To begin with, we suggest that the narratives are taken paragraph by paragraph; first the teacher should read a paragraph aloud, then the students should read it aloud, each perhaps taking a sentence in turn. Then the teacher should test comprehension by translation or questions on the meaning, or a combination of both; questions are useful if the student stumbles. The whole process should move quickly; the students' aim should be to read and understand the Latin at almost the same speed as they read English. In a long narrative it is always possible for the teacher, after reading a paragraph in Latin aloud, to translate it to his students. This does no harm provided the students revise the whole narrative for homework.

The ultimate test of understanding the sense of a passage is for the teacher to read it aloud once or twice while the students do not look at the text, and then test their understanding by comprehension questions or by asking them to tell the story in their own words. As an occasional variant, this exercise is much enjoyed.

Pair work in producing a written translation can be useful, if teachers are willing to allow students to discuss the translation process, though there is a danger that the abler pupil may find himself or herself doing all the work.

Translation is a complex process, not identical with understanding. The acceptable translation must not only be accurate but must express the meaning in natural English. The structure and idiom of Latin is often so different from that of English that word-for-word translation is unacceptable. Students who from the start elicit meaning from whole sentences or paragraphs are more likely to succeed in translating naturally.

Respondē Latīnē exercises

In most chapters the narratives are immediately followed by questions in Latin to be answered in Latin. It is intended that these exercises should be done orally and quickly, and as soon as the narrative is completed. Students must answer with a complete sentence in correct Latin. Some teachers may find that these exercises are too hard for their students and may decide to omit them. In the Commentary below we give only examples of correct answers.

Word-building exercises

From chapter 8 onwards after the narrative comes a short word-building exercise, intended to increase the students' vocabulary without any extra effort of memory. These should be done quickly and orally. The words in these exercises are not included in the General vocabulary unless they occur in the narratives.

Comprehension exercises

Most chapters end with a passage of Latin continuing the story, some of which students are asked to translate; on the rest questions are asked which test the students' understanding without translation. We attach considerable importance to these exercises. They encourage students to read and understand Latin in Latin, which is our ultimate aim. They should be done after the grammar and vocabulary have been learnt. If teachers treat the main narrative orally, they may wish to ask for written answers to these exercises; this will show how fully the students have absorbed new grammar and vocabulary. Most of the questions can be answered by a close understanding of the Latin but we introduce some open-ended questions which ask for a response to the content of the story – the beginning of a critical understanding.

Fābellae

In some chapters there is a playlet, which replaces the comprehension exercise. The purpose of this is to encourage students to read Latin aloud fluently and expressively. You should first read the passage, with different students taking different parts, and make sure it is thoroughly understood, either by translation or questions on the meaning. Then, if time allows, it should be acted by the students.

Grammar and exercises

If the narrative is taken orally and fast, there is a danger that understanding may be vague or incomplete. The exercises, by concentrating on particular points, impose the rigour that is missing in a purely inductive approach. Exercises testing understanding are placed immediately after the grammatical explanation of each point and take various forms: straight translation of Latin sentences, completion exercises, exercises concentrating on verb forms, etc. Most chapters end with an exercise demanding translation of short English sentences into Latin; these are the final test of grammatical understanding and are very useful in the early stages. The exercises are time-consuming and teachers will want to do some, e.g. those on verb forms, orally and quickly.

We do not give a commentary on all the grammar and exercises of every chapter; the grammatical explanations given in the Students' Book are generally sufficient.

Grammatical terminology
For students who know no other language but their own, grammatical terminology will present difficulty; basic concepts such as *verb, noun, sentence, subject, object* must be understood, if grammatical explanations are to make sense to them. But we advise you not to labour this too much to start with; understanding of these terms will gradually sink in.

Sentence patterns
The first two chapters introduce the three basic sentence patterns which form the skeletons of all Latin sentences.

1 subject – verb (intransitive);
2 subject – copula (**est** etc.) – complement;
3 subject – object – verb (transitive).

These skeletons are fleshed out by additions:

1 adjectives agreeing with nouns;
2 adverbs modifying verbs (or less often adjectives);
3 prepositional phrases, i.e. preposition + noun; these are adverbial, modifying verbs;
4 the addition of clauses of two types:
   (a) coordinate, e.g. two main clauses joined by conjunctions such as **et**;
   (b) subordinate, joined to the main clause by a subordinating conjunction, e.g. **ubi** = when.

However complex a sentence may look, it breaks down into these simple units. By the end of Part I these patterns are firmly fixed in the students' minds. It is important that from the start they always deal in whole sentences, not isolated words or phrases.

Inflexion and word order
The meaning of a Latin sentence is determined not by word order, as in English, but by changes in word endings (inflexions). This will gradually become apparent to the student; to drive the point home we sometimes vary the word order.

If we take a simple sentence such as **Scintilla fīliam laudat**, in theory there are five possible arrangements of the words, each with a different emphasis:

1 **Scintilla fīliam laudat**. This is the commonest order; the doer of the action (the subject) comes first and the action (the verb) last.
2 **fīliam Scintilla laudat**. This throws emphasis on **fīliam**, e.g. it's her daughter that Scintilla praises (not her son).
3 **laudat fīliam Scintilla**. This throws emphasis on the action of the verb. 'Scintilla praises her daughter (instead of blaming her).'
4 **Scintilla laudat fīliam**. The emphasis is placed on Scintilla and her daughter rather than on the verb.
5 **laudat Scintilla fīliam**. **laudat** and **fīliam** are more emphatic than **Scintilla**.

All these variations in word order may occur in Latin, but the only variation we use frequently is to place the subject after the verb where the action of the verb requires emphasis.

We labour this point since students simply must watch the endings of words to get the right sense. This they may find unnatural: in English we are apt to pay little attention to word endings, since meaning in English is determined by word order.

We do not suggest that you expatiate on all this to your students; helped by the context, i.e. the meaning demanded by the sense of whole sentences and paragraphs, they will gradually assimilate these principles. But when they go wrong (e.g. they might translate **fīliam Scintilla salutat** as 'her daughter greets Scintilla'), you must always ask them to look at the case endings. They are less likely to go wrong in the context of continuous Latin. This is one reason why in the exercises, as far as possible the separate sentences are linked in meaning.

Analysis
We have not in this revision included exercises in analysis. Although they can be cumbersome and time-consuming, they do force students to concentrate on precise analysis which is, in our view, an essential skill. In case teachers wish to use such exercises we remind them of the notation we suggest: put **s** over subject, **o** over object, **v** over verbs

(**v**+**s** where the subject is in the verb); put **c** over complement; put **io** over indirect object; join adjectives to the nouns they agree with by a hyphen; join prepositions to the nouns they govern by a hyphen; join genitives to the nouns (or adjectives) they depend on with a hyphen; put no mark over adverbs or conjuctions; bracket off subordinate clauses. For example:

$$\overset{s}{\text{Quīntus}} \text{ (ubi ad–patris–agrum accēdit) } \overset{v+s}{\text{Flaccum}} \overset{o}{}$$

$$\overset{v}{\text{vocat}}; \overset{s}{\text{ille}} \overset{v}{\text{in–agrō}} \overset{c}{\text{diū labōrat}} \overset{v}{\text{et fessus est.}}$$

$$\overset{s}{\text{Quīntus}} \overset{o}{\text{cibum}} \overset{io}{\text{patrī}} \overset{v}{\text{trādit.}}$$

This notation does not cover ablative phrases, such as **magnā–vōce**; they need no mark, as they may be classed as adverbial phrases.

Infinitives may be joined to the verbs they depend on, e.g. **dēbētis–labōrāre**.

By the time you come on to the accusative and infinitive construction, analysis of this sort is probably no longer necessary, but you could use the following, e.g.

$$\overset{s}{\text{Horātia}} \overset{v}{\text{dīcit}} \overset{acc.}{\text{puerōs}} \overset{inf.}{\text{dīligenter labōrāre.}}$$

If teachers wish to practise this technique, it can be employed on any of the exercises in which short sentences in Latin are set for translation. And, of course, it can be used orally whenever students are stuck in translation by asking, 'What is the subject?' etc.

Sequence of grammar and syntax in Part I

Chapter 1
Verbs: 1st conjugation, 3rd person singular (he/she).
Nouns and adjectives: nominative singular,
    1st declension.
Syntax: subject – verb; subject – **est** – complement.

Chapter 2
Nouns and adjectives: accusative singular,
    1st declension.
Syntax: subject – object – verb.

Chapter 3
Verbs: 3rd person singular, all conjugations.
Nouns and adjectives: nominative and accusative
    singular, 2nd declension.
Syntax: gender; agreement of adjectives.

Chapter 4
Verbs: 3rd person plural, all conjugations.
Nouns and adjectives: nominative and accusative
    plural, 1st and 2nd declensions.

Chapter 5
Verbs: all persons of present tense, all four
    conjugations.
Nouns and adjectives: ablative case.
Prepositions.

Chapter 6
Verbs: present infinitive, all conjugations; the mixed
    conjugation.*
Nouns: vocative case.
Questions.
    * 3rd conjugation -**iō** verbs (US)

Chapter 7
Verbs: **possum** and **eō**.
Nouns and adjectives: 3rd declension, nom., acc. and
    abl., singular and plural.

Chapter 8
Verbs: imperatives.
Prepositions continued.
Compound verbs.

Chapter 9
Nouns and adjectives: genitive case.
Adverbs.

Chapter 10
Nouns and adjectives: neuters.

Chapter 11
Nouns and adjectives: dative case.

Chapter 12
Review of nouns and adjectives.
Existential **est**; imperatives of **sum**.

Chapter 13
The relative pronoun.
Syntax: subordinate clauses.

Chapter 14
Demonstrative pronouns: **is**, **ille**.
Personal and reflexive pronouns.

Chapter 15
Verbs: **volō**, **nōlō**; irregular imperatives: **dīc**, **dūc**, **fer**, **fac**. Demonstrative pronouns: **hic**, **ipse**.

Chapter 16
Review

The background material

The background material which is placed at the end of every chapter is intended bit by bit to build up a rounded, if incomplete, picture of Rome in the first century BC. We hope that it will both encourage students to acquire some understanding of the civilization within which the literature studied was produced, and develop their ability to observe, abstract and analyse information, paying due regard to evidence, as well as a sympathetic awareness of others' motives and attitudes (GCSE aims **3** and **5** (UK)).

We have followed each essay with questions which we hope will stimulate further thought about the topics raised, especially in the matter of how the civilization of Horace's day relates to the contemporary world. Here, of course, the differences are as important as the similarities. The questions can usually be answered on the basis of the background essays, the Latin story and, of course, the students' own experience. The level of sophistication demanded by these questions varies, and you may wish to omit some if they are too naive or too difficult for your students.

Where a topic appears to have struck a particular chord further reading may be encouraged. Some books recommended for following up topics are:

J. P. V. D. Balsdon: *Life and Leisure in Ancient Rome*, Bodley Head.

J. Boardman, J. Griffin, O. Murray (eds): *The Oxford History of the Classical World*, Oxford.

J. Carcopino: *Daily Life in Ancient Rome*, Penguin.

T. Cornell, J. Matthews: *Atlas of the Roman World*, Phaidon.

O. A. W. Dilke: *The Ancient Romans: How They Lived and Worked*, David and Charles.

M. Hadas: *Imperial Rome*, Time–Life Books.

N. G. L. Hammond, H. H. Scullard (eds): *The Oxford Classical Dictionary*, 2nd edition, Oxford.

P. Jones, K. Sidwell (eds): *The World of Rome*, Cambridge.

U. E. Paoli: *Rome: Its People, Life and Customs*, Longman, repr. Bristol Classical Press.

D. Taylor: *Cicero and Rome*, Macmillan, repr. Bristol Classical Press.

G. I. F. Tingay, J. Badcock: *These Were the Romans*, Hulton Educational.

Our own debt to all of the above in compiling the background sections has been considerable. All are useful sources for additional information on many of the topics, and in the chapter commentaries we have only recommended specific books for additional reading where no very obvious or accessible alternatives exist. We are particularly grateful to Peter Jones and Keith Sidwell for allowing us to see the manuscript of *The World of Rome* (now published); this has made a valuable contribution to our essays.

In our first edition, the opening essays were deliberately pitched at a fairly low level. In their revised form they may sometimes prove too sophisticated for younger students, but the teacher is always there to mediate. The material can be read aloud and discussed in form or set for homework.

Illustrations

The photographic illustrations and reconstructions in the text form an integral part of the course and should be discussed. Comments on them are included in the Commentary below.

Commentary

Title page illustration: this silver statuette of a shepherd carrying a sheep in a bag probably dates from the first century AD. (British Museum, London.)

The introductory sentence is adapted from the opening of Apuleius, *The Golden Ass*; it is translated, but students may be encouraged by seeing at least three Latin words the meaning of which they can guess from English derivatives. With a little help they might see that **vītam** is related to 'vital', **lēctor** to 'lectern', and so they could puzzle out the meaning of each Latin word.

The narratives of the first six chapters centre round daily life in a country town of southern Italy, which in essentials changed remarkably little between the times of Horace and the beginning of this century.

Chapter I

Cartoon captions

See Introduction, p. 5 above.

The following difficulties may arise:

1 the omission of definite and indefinite articles; Latin has no word for 'the' or 'a/an'. The appropriate article must be supplied from the context.

2 the omission of personal pronouns (**labōrat** = she works; **cēnat** = she dines); but if you ask, e.g., 'What is Scintilla doing?' this difficulty disappears. These features of the language need not be discussed until you do the exercises.

The third cartoon shows Scintilla weaving, an activity which may not be familiar to your students; the Roman **māterfamiliās** (mother of the family) regularly spun the wool and wove the cloth to make the family's clothes; compare the epitaph inscribed on a woman's tomb (CIL 1.1007):

casta fuit, domum servāvit, lānam fēcit.

She was faithful to her husband, she kept the house, she spun the wool.

In villages in Italy you can still see women sitting at their doors spinning.

Vocabulary

See Introduction, p. 5 above.

parāta (past participle passive of **parō** = having been prepared): we introduce into the vocabularies a number of past participles passive as ordinary adjectives, e.g. **territus** (8), **commōtus** (12). This causes no difficulty and is a help when we come on to the passive. In chapter 2 a bright student will notice a link between **parāta** and **parat**; if asked about this, it would be sufficient to say at this stage that adjectives can be formed from verbs.

The narrative

See Introduction, p. 6 above.

Grammar and exercises

The first chapter introduces only intransitive verbs of the 1st conjugation (stems in **-a-**) and nouns of the 1st declension (stems in **-a-**). Students should be able to complete the exercises quickly and faultlessly.

Background: Quintus

We suggest that this section should be read fairly speedily. At this stage it is vital to sustain momentum with the language input, and while there are certainly many possible areas for discussion in this passage, there will be ample opportunity to deal with all of them as the course proceeds. The main aim of this section is to bring Horace, the central figure of the course, to life, and to make clear that, whatever liberties we take with the facts of his biography, we are dealing with a real person who lived an extraordinary life in extraordinary times.

A brief discussion of the 'carpe diem' philosophy should summon lively responses from pupils. They should be reminded of the Epicurean recommendation of moderation (penultimate paragraph). Gross over-eating can lead to nasty indigestion.

Sources
Suetonius' 'Life of Horace' from *De viris illustribus* is a key source.
p. 11, paras 1 and 2: Horace's father and his schooling: Horace: *Satires* 1.6.71ff., *Epistles* 2.1.69–71.
p. 12, para. 2: 'I have raised a monument…': Horace: *Odes* 3.30.
p. 12, para. 3: 'When you want a laugh…': Horace: *Epistles* 1.4.15–16.

Question: *carpe diem, quam minimum crēdula posterō*, 'pluck the day (i.e. the day's fruit), trusting as little as possible in the next day' (i.e. make the most of today, since you may not live till tomorrow): Horace: *Odes* 1.11.8.

Illustrations

p. 10: in this relief from the first century BC, the wife sits in a chair with her baby on her knee while her husband reclines. The older children stand on either side. (Musée Calvet, Avignon)
p. 11: this mountainous landscape is characteristic of Apulia in south-east Italy.
p. 12: this relief may be the only reliable ancient portrait of Horace. The wine mug suggests an Epicurean and the receding hairline suggests Horace! (Museum of Fine Arts, Boston)

Chapter 2

Cartoon captions

These introduce transitive verbs with direct objects; you should draw attention to the changes in noun endings – nominative -a, accusative -am. You might ask your students why they think the endings change. Do not at this stage attempt to explain the ablative (**in casā**).

What do the following sentences mean?

4   Latin does not express 'his', 'her', etc. if the reference is obvious, except to give emphasis, e.g. **Scintilla fīliam suam laudat** means: Scintilla praises her own daughter.

In this sentence the word order changes: object (**fīli-am**), verb (**salūtat**), subject (**Scintill-a**). The sooner students grasp that in Latin sense depends on word-ending, not word order, the better. The effect of placing the object **fīliam** first word is to throw greater emphasis onto it, e.g.

fīliam laudat Scintilla, fīlium culpat.
Her daughter Scintilla praises, her son she blames.

Argus steals the dinner

2   **intrat** is used intransitively in chapter 1 (**Horātia in casam intrat** = Horatia enters into the house), but transitively here (**casam intrat**). Both usages are common.
5   **laeta**: Latin uses the adjective since 'happy' describes Horatia herself rather than how she listens; English idiom uses the adverb 'happily'.

Argus: this word introduces a noun with a new nominative ending, but since it is a proper name this should not cause difficulty and requires no comment at this stage. You may remind students that as a general rule capital letters are only used at the beginning of proper names.
6   **eam rapit et dēvorat**: eam is feminine because it refers to **cēna** (if students translate as 'her', you will have to make this point).

dēvorat: the word is neither glossed nor in the chapter vocabulary, since the context and the English derivative (devours) make the meaning clear. See Introduction, p. 5 above.

Respondē Latīnē

See Introduction, p. 6 above.
1   Scintilla cēnam parat.
2   Horātia aquam in casam portat.
3   Argus casam intrat.
4   Scintilla īrāta est quod Argus cēnam dēvorat.

Grammar and exercises

The only new grammar is the accusative singular of the 1st declension, but the important concept of inflexion is introduced with the change **puell-a** nom., **puell-am** acc.

It may help to point out that English was once an inflected language and that a very few of these inflexions still survive, e.g. I (subject) help him (object); he (subject) helps me (object). You might ask your students what is wrong with these English sentences:

Us are helping he. Him don't help we.
Why are they wrong? This could lead to a discussion of subject, object and case, and then to the terms nominative and accusative.

More grammatical terms are introduced into this chapter than into any other, and younger students cannot be expected to grasp their meaning clearly straight away, but they will gradually assimilate them.

Exercise 2.1
Students should be asked how they arrive at their answers, e.g. **Horātia** – subject; **Scintillam** – object.
1   Do not explain that **casā** is in the ablative case unless students ask you; the phrase is unlikely to cause difficulty; the use of prepositions + ablative is not explained until chapter 5.
4   **fīlia**: students should be encouraged to translate as 'her daughter'. Latin does not often use personal adjectives except for emphasis, unless the reference is unclear. Students should be encouraged to use them in English when the context requires them, e.g. in 6.

Exercise 2.3
1   'into the house': you may get the answer **in casā** and will have to stress that *in* = 'into' is followed by the accusative (as in English 'we bumped into *him*').

11

Background: Women

A brief but important summary of modern views on Roman women can be found in G.Clark: *Women in the Ancient World*, New Surveys in the Classics 21, Oxford. Valuable and stimulating material can also be found in E. Fantham, P. Foley, N. B. Kampen, S. B. Pomeroy, H. A. Shapiro: *Women in the Classical World*, Oxford.

Clearly this section will provide a rich field for exploration. The second question should certainly be discussed at some length.

What 'image' of Roman women emerges from p. 15 to p. 16, para. 2? How acceptable does that image seem today?

p. 16, para. 2 makes it clear that most girls married very early by our standards. What are the pupils' responses to that? (Cicero betrothed his daughter Tullia at the age of nine; she had been married three times when she died aged thirty.) And what do they feel about arranged marriages? Do they agree with our assertion that there is no reason to believe that these usually led to an unsuccessful marriage (last sentence of para. 2)?

Responses should be invited to the second half of p. 16, para. 4 ('Weaving is a skilful and creative craft ... and giving mutual support and practical help').

How impressed are pupils by the more positive aspects of Roman women's lives dealt with on p. 17, paras 2 and 3?

Sources

p. 15, para 1: we have made use of the idealized picture of the chaste Roman wife in Virgil: *Aeneid* 8.408–13.
p. 16, para. 3: 'To Urbana': CIL 6.29580, Rome.
'This woman': Philematio, wife of the butcher L. Aurelius Hermia, from the Viminal Hill in Rome. Cl. Etr. 2.959.
Question 1: quotation from Horace: *Odes* 3.24.19.

Illustrations

p. 14: this famous mosaic of a dog is from the floor of a doorway in Pompeii. (National Museum of Archaeology, Naples)
p. 15: on this black-figure lekythos by the Amasis Painter, dating from 550–540 BC, are some of the processes of wool-making. Here we see the loom with two women working at it. To the right of it a woman is holding scales in which the raw wool (almost out of frame) is being weighed. On the left a woman draws a 'snake' of wool from a basket. The unrelated scene on the rim shows a goddess or priestess to whom young men and dancing girls are paying homage. (Metropolitan Museum of Art, New York)
p. 17: this beautiful scene of hairdressing from a wall-painting by a Campanian painter of the first century BC shows a girl being prepared for initiation into the rites of Bacchus. (Villa of the Mysteries, Pompeii)

Chapter 3

Cartoon captions

The captions are unlikely to cause difficulty. Students may notice two points:
1 the verb ending **-t** indicates the 3rd person (he/she), whether the preceding vowel is **-a** or **-i**; this will be confirmed by a quick look at the verbs in the vocabulary (which includes **-e** verbs – **manet**, **sedet**, **videt**).
2 the accusative ends **-m** for both types of noun (e.g. **casa-m**, **agru-m**).

They may well ask about the noun ending **agr-ō** (caption 1); if they understand the meaning of the phrase, it is better not to embark on an explanation of the ablative case yet (it is explained in chapter 5); until then occurrences of **in** + ablative are glossed in the narrative.

Vocabulary

In the vocabulary, the adjective **ānxius, -a, -um** is given with all gender endings. You should say that **ānxius** is used in referring to a man or boy, **ānxia** in referring to a woman or girl and **ānxium** in referring to a thing. Although this is not strictly correct it is a good preparation for the discussion of gender in the grammatical notes, and in reading the narrative it will save any hiccough over, e.g. **Flaccus fessus est** (they have learnt this adjective in Vocabulary 1 as **fessa**).

Quintus helps his father

In the narrative the following prepositional phrases occur: **ad agrum, in agrō, ad eum, in terrā, ad terram**; in the comprehension exercise: **in hortum, in casā, in casam, in agrō**. Those with the ablative are glossed. Bright students are likely to notice the difference in meaning between **in** + acc. and **in** + abl.; if so, you will have to give an explanation, but there is no need to use the term 'ablative' yet.
3 **sēcum**: 'with him'; this phrase may raise questions since students learn in this vocabulary that **eum** = him. The reflexive pronoun **sē** is used because 'him' refers back to **puer**, subject of the sentence (if **cum eō** were used, **eō** would refer to someone other than **puer**). **cum** is tacked onto the personal pronouns to produce **mēcum, tēcum, sēcum**, etc. The phrase **sēcum** occurs quite frequently and sooner or later you may have to give an explanation, but don't explain unless asked.

4 **Flaccum videt et vocat**: Latin says 'He sees and calls Flaccus', English 'He sees Flaccus and calls him'; the object **Flaccum** precedes and belongs to both verbs. English and Latin idiom here differ; your students must always be encouraged to use natural English, which they will do if they understand whole sentences together.

7 **olīvās**: Latin uses the same word for both the tree and the fruit. Olives were a vital component of the economy of the ancient world; they were not only eaten but used to provide scent, cooking oil and light. The first pressing was used in the manufacture of scent, the second for cooking, the third as fuel in oil lights.

8 **lāpsat Quīntus**: the verb precedes the subject, which throws greater emphasis on the action of the verb. Latin uses this word order freely and your students must become familiar with it.

Respondē Latīnē

1   Quīntus in agrō manet quod Flaccum iuvat.
2   Quīntus olīvam ascendit et olīvās dēcutit*.
3   Flaccus ānxius est quod Quīntus ad terram cadit.

    *You will have to give them this word.

English derivatives

E.g. agriculture, porter, labour, puerile, video, filial, audience, amble, consume, olive, ascend, anxious. This exercise can be used on any vocabulary.

Flaccus Quintum laudat

This is the first comprehension exercise: see the Introduction, p. 8 above.

1 **domum**: '(to) home'. **domum** will appear to your students to be the object of **redit**; if asked, you will have to explain that the preposition, e.g. **ad**, is omitted with **domum** (just as it is with 'home' in English).

The grammatical terms necessary for answering question 4 may cause difficulty at this stage; either omit the question or do it orally after your students have studied the grammar. We do not ask such grammatical questions on the other comprehension exercises; if you think your students need such questions to tighten up their grammar, you can easily make some up on other exercises.

Grammar and exercises

This chapter probably contains as much grammatical difficulty as any other in Part I, since it introduces three alien concepts – declension, conjugation and gender. But the difficulties lie more in grammatical terminology and theory than in practical understanding of the Latin in a context. You should try, therefore, not to get too

bogged down in explanations, but we append these notes in case bright students ask too many questions.

Declension
The whole concept of nouns belonging to different groups called declensions will be alien to your students. They must accept it as a feature of the language, but if they insist on an explanation, you could say at this stage that nouns (and adjectives) decline differently according to their stem ending; their stem can end in any of the five vowels or in a consonant, so that they will eventually find that there are, properly speaking, six declensions: stems ending **a** (1st declension), in **o** (2nd), in consonant (3rd), in **i** (3rd), in **u** (4th) and in **e** (5th). The trouble here is that in the 2nd declension **o** has been replaced in classical Latin by **u** in nominative and accusative, so any explanation at this stage, except in broad outline, becomes complicated. A glance at the charts of nouns in the Reference grammar (p. 145) might help (the ablative singular shows the principle most clearly, but remember that your students have not yet learnt the ablative).

declension	abl. sing.	characteristic
1st or A decl.	puell-Ā	Ā
2nd or O decl.	colon-Ō	Ō
3rd or I decl.*	mar-Ī	Ī
3rd or consonant decl.	reG-e	consonant
4th or U decl.	grad-Ū	Ū
5th or E decl.	r-Ē	Ē

*Originally I stems had acc. sing. **-im** and abl. sing. **-ī**.

Conjugation
Students should notice (1) that although the stem vowel changes in the different conjugations, the person ending (**-t**) is the same for all; (2) that in the 3rd conjugation (stems in consonants), a vowel (**i**) is inserted before the person ending.

Students might expect six conjugations, corresponding to the five vowels + consonants. No Latin verbs have stems in **o**; there are verbs with stems ending **u** but these are classed with the 3rd (consonant) conjugation.

Exercise 3.2
This is the first exercise in which verbs are used with no subject expressed, i.e. the subject is 'in the verb', but instances have appeared freely in the narratives. Out of context there is obviously no way of telling whether **audit** = 'he hears' or 'she hears'.

Gender
This is, perhaps, the hardest piece of grammatical explanation so far, though it will not cause much

difficulty to those who have learnt some French or Spanish.

You should pass over the neuter as lightly as possible; neuter nouns are not learnt until chapter 10, although to save trouble later, adjectives are always given with all three genders, in the abbreviated form: **magn-us**, **-a**, **-um**.

Background: Slaves and freedmen

A valuable summary of modern attitudes to slavery is given in T. Wiedemann: *Slavery in Greece and Rome*, New Surveys in the Classics 19, Oxford.

In this background section there is much room for discussion and exploration. The appalling insecurity of the slave's lot (p. 20, para. 3–p. 21, para. 1) could be counterbalanced with important compensations (p. 21, para. 2–p. 22, para. 2). Do the latter provide any kind of 'justification' for the system? We hope that it will not smack of cultural fascism if we say that we very much hope that the answer which ultimately emerges from your pupils will be a resounding No!

The possibilities open to freedmen need discussion (p. 22, paras 3–5). The extraordinary social mobility of the Roman world, from which Horace himself was so conspicuously to benefit, should be emphasized here. But is a patronage system demeaning for the individual who is patronized as well as corrupting for the patron?

Emphasis should perhaps be put on our balancing of Juvenal's racism with the Romans' openness with the gift of citizenship (p. 23, para. 2).

Sources

p. 21, para. 1: Vedius Pollio: Seneca: *De ira* 3.40, Dio Cassius: 54.23.1ff. Dio tells how Augustus, who was dining with Pollio when he gave this command, ordered the rest of his crystal cups to be smashed, and Pollio did not dare go through with the punishment. When Pollio died soon afterwards, Augustus had his house razed to the ground.

Hadrian: Galen: *Diseases of the Mind* 4 (Kuhn 5117). Cato the Elder: A. E. Astin: *Cato the Censor*, Oxford, App. 12.

p. 22, para. 2: Seneca: *Epistles* 47.1.10.

p. 23, para. 2: Juvenal: *Satires* 3.62–3.

para. 3: C. Julius Mygdonius inscription: Dessau 1980.

Illustrations

p. 19: this fine black-figure Attic vase from the sixth century BC shows a boy picking up olives which three men are beating from the branches of an olive tree. (British Museum, London)

p. 23: these two freedmen were formerly slaves of P. Licinius. At the top (in the pediment) are blacksmiths' tools: hammer, anvil and tongs. To the right are carpenters' tools: a drill with the bow used to rotate it, a marking knife, an adze and a short-bladed chisel. To the left are the fasces, the axe and the rod used in the ceremony of freeing the slave. (British Museum, London)

Chapter 4

Cartoon captions

The cartoons make the meaning of these captions self-evident. The concept of number (singular and plural) is easily grasped, since both noun and verb endings change in English to indicate difference in number, although adjectives do not change in English – you might in passing call attention to this in captions five and six.

Scintilla and Horatia at the fountain

The wealthier houses in Pompeii did have a piped water supply but most houses had none. And so one daily chore for the women of a family was to go to one of the public fountains which were dotted round the town and draw water. Here they would meet their friends and chat. The same was true in ancient Greece, a scene frequently represented in Athenian vase paintings, and it was also true in modern Italy until quite recently.

4 **colloquium**: **colloquium** is neuter. We use 2nd declension neuter nouns freely in the accusative, where the ending is the same as that of masculine nouns. We advise you not to comment on this.

8 **eam**: 'it'. Since **urna** is feminine the pronoun **eam**, referring to **urnam**, is also feminine. Students should be warned of this.

11 **surge**; 12 **portā**; 16 **manē**: the imperative, the form of the verb giving orders, is explained in chapter 8. All imperative forms occurring before that are glossed.

14 **lūdum**: **lūdus** means (1) play, game, sport (**lūdī** = the public 'games', which included gladiatorial combats and dramatic performances); (2) a school (usually an elementary school).

16 **Quīnte**: vocative case; this is explained in chapter 6. Explain to students, if necessary, but it can probably be passed over without comment.

Respondē Latīnē

1 Horātia urnam aegrē portat quod magna est.
2 Horātia lāpsat; urna ad terram cadit.
3 Horātia ad casam redit quod Scintilla 'aliam urnam' inquit 'ā casā portā*.'

* It is hard to give an answer to this question without using an imperative – you will have to give this to your students.

Flaccus goes to the pub

As in modern Italy, so in ancient, there were numerous drinking shops scattered round the towns; see illustration on p. 28. The names of Flaccus' friends and the tenor of their talk are lifted from Petronius, *Satyricon* 42ff.

3 **bibit**: we do not gloss this word; its meaning must be deduced from the context.

5 **pluit** has the same form for present and perfect; the sense here requires a perfect. You may have to say something about tenses, if asked, although the word is glossed, but don't delay over it.

7 **duovirī**: the **duovirī** were the two magistrates elected each year in all *colōniae* (see the background essay in this chapter).

Grammar and exercises

ille, illa

The demonstrative pronoun **ille** is used both as a true pronoun in place of a noun and as an adjective, e.g. **ille colōnus** = 'that farmer'. In the following exercise we use it only as a pronoun. In exercise 4.5, tell your students to make clear in their translations who **ille** etc. refers to.

Background: The country town: Venusia

The information given in this background section is largely self-contained and factual. The importance of the town of Venusia should be stressed. In addition to what is said about it in the Students' book, the town put up a resistance to Hannibal and provided hospitality for nearly 10,000 fugitives after the Battle of Cannae in 216 BC (Livy 22.54). A promising field for exploration is the evocation of what life was like in a Roman country town. The sense of a diverse but unified community – with its mixture of farmers and townsfolk (page 29, para. 2) – should not prove too difficult to convey.

But the main opportunity for discussion here is provided by the illustrations of Pompeii (see below). The archaeological remains of Venusia itself are rudimentary. A good modern book on Pompeii is Andrew Wallace-Hadrill: *Houses and Society in Pompeii and Herculaneum*, Princeton. A CD-Rom is available through standard suppliers called 'Exploring Ancient Cities', which includes splendid material on Pompeii.

Sources
p. 29, para. 3: 'boys who were the descendants...':
Horace: *Satires* 1.6.73–4.
para. 4: Virgil quotation: *Georgics* 2.157–8.

Illustrations

p. 26: in this black-figure vase of about 530 BC from Vulci, some women are coming to a spring with a lion head spout to fill their vases. The central figure is leaving after filling hers. There is an element of humour since the jar on which the scene is painted is itself a water jar. (Villa Giulia Museum, Rome)

pp. 27–8: in these photographs of Pompeii can be seen (1) stepping stones across a street and the ruts made by wagon wheels; (2) the forum, the most perfect surviving example of a Roman central square, the Temple of Jupiter with its Corinthian columns above fifteen steps, and looming over them Mount Vesuvius with its dramatic crater (1277 metres). It was the eruption of this volcano on 24 August 79 AD which buried the city under a layer of pumice-stone and then one of ashes and thus preserved it for the modern world; (3) a pub (*thermopōlium*) on the Via dell'Abbondanza which served hot and cold drinks from the counter; (4) an election poster from Pompeii inviting support for Cnaeus Helvius Sabinus.

p. 29: this hill town is Barrea l'Aquila in the Abruzzi in Italy.

Chapter 5

Cartoon captions

Although all persons of the verb are introduced in these captions, they do not cause difficulty. In this particular case, before reading the story, it might pay to ask students to write out all persons of a verb, e.g. **labōrō**. Ask them to list the persons – I, you (sing.), he/she, we, you (pl.), they – and to write the Latin forms opposite, deducing the answers from the captions.

Vocabulary

In this vocabulary we still give verbs in the 3rd person singular to make clear which conjugation they belong to; in chapter 6 the infinitive is learnt and from then on verbs are given as, e.g. **clāmō, clāmāre; dīcō, dīcere**.

trēs: students might ask why this adjective is given with only two genders. The reason is that masculine and feminine have the same form (**trēs** belongs to the 3rd declension).

nec/neque: **nec** is used before consonants, **neque** when the following word starts with a vowel or h. Latin never says **et ... nōn**; thus in line 14 of the narrative **lāna bona est nec cāra** = the wool is good and not dear. You will need to explain this difference in idiom when you meet it.

Market day

Markets were held every ninth day and were public holidays. People attended the market not only for buying and selling but to meet their friends; market day was an important social occasion. In a country town they would be held in the forum, the city centre.

1 **nūndinae sunt**: although **nūndinae** is singular in meaning, it is plural in form; so we have **nūndinae sunt** = it is market day. Students may be warned, if they ask, that they will meet a number of words which in Latin are plural in form but singular in meaning, e.g. **epulae** = a feast.

4 **parāta es?**: as in English, questions are sometimes expressed simply by tone of voice, without an interrogative particle.

6 **Flaccus lānam portat, Scintilla olīvās, Horātia ficōs**: the verb **portat** governs all three nouns in the accusative; this should be clear enough but may cause a stumble.

6–7 **ad forum**: markets could be held in any big enough space; the **forum** was one obvious venue and we assume that this was used in Venusia.

9 **tabernae**: these stalls were flimsy constructions erected for the day (like the stalls in English markets). Flaccus would in fact have had to carry the stall as well as the bag of wool to market.

mercēs: 'wares'; accusative plural 3rd declension; so also in lines 12 and 23 (this probably requires no comment).

15 **tribus dēnāriīs**: 'for three denarii'. The ablative case is used to express price, the genitive to express value; so in lines 17–18 **quantī olīvae sunt?**, '(of) how much are the olives?' Both phrases are glossed and you need not explain this yet.

24 **vendidimus**: sense here demands a perfect form; this is likely to raise questions and you are bound to explain that Latin indicates changes of tense by altering the endings of verbs, but students should recognize the person ending **-mus**. The same problem will occur in the last sentence of the playlet, with **cēnābimus**.

The prices demanded by Flaccus and family are given in terms of *dēnāriī* and are excessively high. There were 18 *assēs* in a *dēnārius*; a basket of figs would scarcely have cost an *as*, and we learn from Horace that the fees at the school of Flavius were 8 *assēs* a month – see next chapter. But we wished to avoid using 3rd declension forms. Students may be amused to learn that in our own old coinage we still counted in *dēnāriī* – 1*d* etc.

Fābella: To the fish stall

On playlets, see Introduction, pp. 6–7 above.

Some 3rd declension nouns could not be avoided in this exercise – **piscātor** and **piscēs**; **piscātor** occurs only in the nominative and vocative singular and will cause no problem. But **piscēs** occurs both as nominative and accusative plural and you may have to give a quick explanation of this.

The last sentence contains two verbs in the future tense (**cēnābimus, erit**); these are glossed and students will note that the person endings (**-mus, -t**) are the same as those of the present.

Grammar and exercises

Verbs

The amount of grammar in this chapter may look formidable, but stress to your students that the person endings are the same for all conjugations and that these are simply added to the stem vowel in conjugations 1, 2 and 4. In the 3rd (consonant) conjugation a vowel is inserted before the person endings (**i**). Tell them to note especially the forms **reg-Unt** and **audi-Unt**, in which there is an unexpected change of vowel.

Make sure that they read aloud the present tenses of **regō** and **audiō** with correct vowel lengths (**i** is short throughout in the present of **regō**, but it is long in the forms **audīs, audīmus, audītis**).

Latin only expresses subject pronouns for emphasis, e.g. **ego labōrō, tū lūdis**: *I* am working, *you* are playing.

The ablative case

Apart from its use after prepositions, other uses of the ablative occasionally occur in the narrative but these are glossed, e.g. **posterō diē, magnā vōce**. In chapter 12, the meanings of the ablative case are summarized in the traditional formula 'by, with or from', and its uses are dealt with more fully in Part II (chapter 22). Teachers may wish to comment on common uses earlier as they occur.

Prepositions

Prepositions have been used freely from the start. When the ablative has been learnt, students must learn carefully which case each takes. This is not hard but requires frequent revision.

Background:
The Roman farmer – and market day

The idealization of the rustic life (p. 34, para. 1 and p. 35, para. 1) is important. Horace himself gives scope to this theme in his poetry, most famously in the town and country mouse episode from *Satires* 2.6.79–117 (finely translated by N. Rudd in *Horace, Satires and Epistles; Persius, Satires*, Penguin). Virgil's *Georgics*, while at times treating country life with a grim realism, can espouse the dream of an idyllic rustic existence, and we have included his picture of the Cilician old man (p. 35, para. 1) to stimulate discussion of the credibility of such descriptions. Comparisons with the English Romantics, especially Wordsworth, may prove helpful here.

In p. 35, para. 2 we describe a Roman market day. Pupils with experience of modern markets can be invited to comment on similarities and differences here. An obvious contrast is provided by the impersonal efficiency of today's hypermarkets.

p. 36, para. 2 gives further evidence of the terrible nature of one aspect of slave labour. This deserves discussion. Forced labour under Hitler and Stalin provides two twentieth-century points of reference for the use of human beings as dispensable machines.

The question points pupils to the contrasts and similarities between farming methods in the modern and ancient world. What difference has mechanization made? How much dogged effort is there now left in farming? Huge modern farms may well bring to mind the *latifundia* (vast country estates – final paragraph) of the Roman world.

J. P. V. D. Balsdon: *Life and Leisure in Ancient Rome*, Bodley Head, and P. Jones and K. Sidwell (eds): *The World of Rome*, Cambridge, are particularly helpful here.

Sources
p. 34, para. 4: the farmer's calendar is from Balsdon: *Life and Leisure in Ancient Rome*, p. 59.
p. 35, para. 1: Virgil on the pirate from Cilicia: *Georgics* 4.125–33.
para. 2: Virgil's peasant Simylus: *Moretum* 81–2.
p. 36, para. 2: Varro quotation: *De re rustica* 1.17.1.5–7.

Illustrations

pp. 32–3: the monkeys in this market scene are perhaps intended to attract custom.
p. 33 and front cover: in this mosaic from Pompeii there can be seen a pattern consisting of more than twenty species of fish, crustacea and other marine creatures including an extremely realistic octopus. (National Museum of Archaeology, Naples)
p. 34: this scene of two satyrs – note their tails – treading grapes probably dates from the second century AD. (Archaeological Museum, Venice)
p. 35: this frieze of the Augustan period shows women selling fruit at a shop which also sells poultry. (Ostia Museum)
p. 36: in this section of the Travaux Champêtre mosaic, the man to the left is ploughing while the man to the right is sowing. (Cherchelle, Algeria)

Chapter 6

Cartoon captions

The prolative infinitive after verbs such as 'I want' should cause no difficulty to the student. The context will probably make clear the meaning of **iubet** and **cupiunt**; you may have to give the meaning of **dēbētis** and **cōnstituit**.

Vocabulary

You should emphasize that the infinitives of 2nd conjugation verbs have long **ē** (e.g. **dēbēre**), those of 3rd conjugation verbs have short **e** (e.g. **lūdere**). There is no example of a 4th conjugation verb in the vocabulary (**eō**, **īre** and **exeō**, **exīre** are irregular, which may cause some confusion), but there is one of the mixed conjugation – **cupiō**, **cupere**; you might have to explain this briefly before the grammar is studied. The only other mixed conjugation verb in the narrative is **facit** (line 3).

The school of Flavius

Horace wrote (*Satires* 1.6.72–6): 'My father did not want to send me to the school of Flavius, where the big boys, sons of big centurions, went with their satchels and tablets hung over their left shoulders, taking their eight asses on the Ides of each month.' However, we take the liberty of making Flaccus send Quintus to Flavius' school for his elementary education, although he removes him later to take him to Rome (see Part II, chapter 18). The local school was cheap; the children took the fee themselves to Flavius; they had no tutor to carry their satchels and tablets.

We make Flavius' school co-educational; there is evidence that girls sometimes attended elementary schools (see E. Fantham *et al.*, *Women in the Classical World*, Oxford, pp. 272–3.).
2 **prior**: 'first', i.e. before Quintus. The usual word for 'first' is **prīmus**, but **prior** (a comparative adjective) is used when only two persons are concerned.

quae: in Part I, the relative pronoun is used freely in the nominative, always glossed; as its nominative plural is the same as that of e.g. **puell-ae**, it is unlikely to cause difficulty here.
3–4 **puellā ... pulchrā** is in the ablative case since it is in apposition to **Iūliā**. Students may notice this; if they don't, don't comment at this stage.

valdē: 'very'; this has occurred three times and we cease to gloss it.
7 **Gāī**: vocative case (see Grammar).
11 **labōrāre**: infinitive because it depends on **cupiunt**: 'the girls (want) to work'.
20 **ad sē**: the reflexive pronoun **sē** is used, referring

back to the subject of the verb, **magister**; it is glossed – don't comment.

21 **asinus**: 'an ass'; this is not glossed.

errās: the first meaning of **errō** is 'I wander, stray'; then 'I stray from the truth, err' (cf. Book of Common Prayer, General Confession: 'We have erred, and strayed from thy ways like lost sheep').

25 **labōrant puerī**: the subject follows the verb, throwing emphasis on how hard they are working.

Respondē Latīnē

1 Horātia prior ad lūdum advenit, quod festīnat, sed Quīntus lentē prōcēdit.

2 magister īrātus est, quod Quīntus et Gāius sērō adveniunt.

3 magister dīcit: 'Decime, asinus es,' quod ille litterās nōn rēctē scrībit.

4 Decimus respondet: 'errās, magister. litterās rēctē scrībō.'

Flavius decides to tell a story

8–9 **diū scrībimus**: 'we have been writing for a long time'. If an action begins in the past and continues up to the present, Latin uses the present tense (the so-called 'present of remaining effects'). Don't labour this point; a good student might be guided by the context to give a correct translation.

10 **puerī** can mean 'children' as well as 'boys'.

11 **volō**: whereas **cupiō** = 'I positively desire to', **volō** usually means 'I am willing to'.

Grammar and exercises

Infinitives

The infinitive presents no difficulty at this stage, since its usage appears to be similar to that of English. You might need to remark that its form never changes.

The mixed conjugation

These verbs are partly 3rd and partly 4th (they are sometimes called 3rd conjugation -**iō** verbs). The infinitive must be carefully learnt.

cap-is, **cap-imus**, **cap-itis**: note that **i** is short in these forms (like **reg-is**, **reg-imus**, **reg-itis**, not like **audī-s**, **audī-mus**, **audī-tis**).

There are only twelve verbs of this conjugation of which the commonest are: **capiō**, **cupiō**, **rapiō** ('I seize'), **faciō**, **iaciō**, **fugiō**, (**cōn**)**spiciō** ('I catch sight of'); deponent verbs (see Part III, chapter 36) include **gradior** and compounds, **patior**, **morior**.

Exercise 6.2

4 (**lūdō**): students will be inclined to write **lūdimus**; point out that it depends on **cupimus**. So also in 5,

students might say **audīmus**; they must be clear that both 'sit' and 'listen to' depend on 'we must'.

The vocative case

This presents no difficulty once the 2nd declension forms are known. 'ō' is used with the vocative to express strong emotion.

Questions

Questions have been used freely from the start. They present no difficulty in the simplified form we present here except for the use of -**ne**; the idea of attaching this particle to the first word in the sentence may seem strange to students.

We omit at this stage **num**, said to introduce questions expecting the answer 'No', e.g. **num fessus es**? 'Surely you are not tired?' It is not in fact at all common. We also omit at present **utrum ... an** used in double questions, e.g. **utrum laetus es an trīstis**? 'Are you happy or sad?'

Exercise 6.6

This is a revision exercise.

5 **iubet**: the English verb 'tell' has several meanings: (1) I report – 'tell me what happened', Latin **nārrō**; (2) I order, as here, Latin **iubeō**; (3) I utter – 'I told a lie', Latin **dīcō**. Latin uses a different verb for each meaning. It is worth pointing this out to students as a warning against attempting one-for-one translation; they must think of the meaning.

6 **ad fontem**: since the 3rd declension accusative **fontem** occurred several times in the narrative of chapter 4, students are unlikely to be bothered by this phrase, but you may have to remind them.

Background: Education

Among the possible areas for discussion here are:

Did it matter that Roman girls dropped out of the educational system after the primary stage (p. 40, para. 1 and p. 42, para. 3)?

For educated Romans, Greek was a second language (p. 40, para. 2 and p. 42, para. 1). Why Greek? What is the second language for your pupils? Why is it that language?

Do your pupils feel that teaching methods have changed much since Roman times (p. 41, paras 1 and 2)?

How useful a skill is arithmetic (Horace quotation on p. 41, para. 1)?

The Romans had no scientific education but brought their civilization to all the Western world. Do your pupils feel that an arts education is a more valuable preparation for life than a scientific one (p. 42, paras 1–2)?

How important is the study of (a) music and (b)

astronomy? A valuable book on this subject is R. Barrow: *Greek and Roman Education*, Macmillan.

Sources

p. 40, para. 2: carrying their satchels and taking along the schoolmaster's pay once a month: Horace: *Satires* 1.6.73–4.

his father took him there: Horace: *Satires* 1.6.81–2.

p. 41, para. 1: the quotation is from Horace: *Ars poetica* 325–31.

para. 2: the quotation is from Martial: *Epigrams* 9.68.1–4.

p. 42, para. 1: the quotation is from Horace: *Epistles* 2.1.156.

Question 2: Pliny on a good school: *Letters* 3.3.

Illustrations

p. 38: in this marble relief from Gaul dating from about 200 AD, two boys sit on *sellae* on either side of the teacher with papyrus *volūmina* unrolled; a third arrives late, carrying his *capsula*. (Rheinisches Landesmuseum, Trier)

p. 39: back row: four leaves of a wooden writing tablet; inkpots in faience, pottery and bronze; front row: a letter in Greek on papyrus; (from the front) a reed pen, a bronze pen, an ivory stylus and a bronze stylus. (British Museum, London)

pp. 40–1: a marble relief from the second century AD. From left to right: suckling the baby; the father holds his child, accepting him into the family; the boy at play rides a toy chariot drawn by a donkey; he receives instruction from his father. The (incomplete) inscription lists the names of the monument's dedicator and dedicatees (Louvre Museum, Paris)

Chapter 7

The narratives of chapters 7–12 form a digression in which Flavius tells in outline the stories of the *Iliad* and *Aeneid*. The story of the *Iliad* would have been known to all Roman children and a knowledge of it is essential to an understanding of most Latin poetry. In telling the story of the *Aeneid*, Flavius anticipates Virgil by forty years, but the legend that Aeneas, son of Venus and Anchises, and a prince of Troy, escaped from the burning city with his father and son and after many wanderings founded a city from which Rome sprung, had been known to Romans for many years; it had been developed by, amongst others, Virgil's great predecessor Ennius (239–169 BC) in his historical epic the *Annals*. It appealed to the Romans' sense of patriotism by placing Rome's founder firmly in the great cycle of Greek legends at a time when Rome was falling more and more under Greek influence.

Cartoon captions

These should give no trouble, but you may like to call attention to the 3rd declension case endings – **can-em**, **patr-em**, **can-e**, **comit-ēs**, **comit-ibus**. When students come to study the grammar, they will find a difficulty in the fact that the nominative and accusative plural have the same ending; this can cause real ambiguity and confusion, which can only be solved by clinging to the sense demanded by the context.

Vocabulary

We use the customary abbreviations in listing genitives of nouns and nominative of adjectives; you may need to explain these. We do not abbreviate 3rd declension nouns and adjectives.

Flavius' story: The siege of Troy

The theme of the *Iliad* is stated in the first line of the whole poem: 'Sing goddess, of the wrath of Achilles…' The quarrel between Agamemnon and Achilles occurred in the tenth year of the siege of Troy, when Agamemnon took from Achilles his prize, the girl Briseis. When his honour was thus insulted, Achilles refused to fight any longer. This sets in motion the whole plot of the *Iliad*. When he and his men no longer fight, the Greeks are driven back to their ships, and in Book 9 Agamemnon sends an embassy of Achilles' friends, offering reparation and asking him to come to the rescue. Achilles refuses but is persuaded by his dearest friend Patroclus to allow him to go into battle wearing Achilles' armour. Patroclus is killed in battle by the greatest Trojan hero, Hector, son of King Priam. Then at last Achilles' anger is turned from Agamemnon against the Trojans. He leads his men into battle and sweeps the Trojans off the field into the city. Hector alone challenges him and is slain in single combat.

You might like to read to your students a translation of part of the magnificent first book of the *Iliad*.

1 **Mycēnārum**: genitive plural (**Mycēnae** and many other places are plural in form). The genitive case is not learned until chapter 9 but it is no longer possible to exclude it; all occurrences are glossed in this and the next chapter.

Mycenae, in the north-east of the Peloponnese, was according to tradition the richest and most powerful of the kingdoms of late Bronze Age Greece. The tradition is supported by archaeology which has revealed an immensely strong and wealthy fortress complex. In the *Iliad* Agamemnon is the acknowledged leader of the other kings. Your students might like to do some research on the Trojan War, which many modern scholars believe to have been an historical event, resulting in the destruction of Troy VIIa in about 1220 BC.

2 **in Trōiānōs**: 'against the Trojans'; **in** + acc. can have a hostile force.

3 **Achillēs**: son of the sea nymph Thetis and Peleus, Achilles was the bravest and strongest of the Greek heroes; his father was king in Thessaly, in north-east Greece.

4 **Ulixēs** = Ulysses, identified with the Greek hero Odysseus, whose return from Troy to Ithaca is the subject of Homer's *Odyssey*. Ithaca is a small island off the west coast of Greece; Odysseus' contribution to the expedition in manpower was small but he was famous for his cunning (it was he who proposed the strategy of the wooden horse, which led to the capture of Troy).

5 **urbem Trōiam**: Latin says 'the city Troy', Troy being in apposition to city, but English says 'the city of Troy', a difference in idiom which should be noted.

7 **decem annōs**: 'for ten years'; Latin expresses duration of time by the accusative without a preposition. As the accusative case has been met only as the direct object and after certain prepositions, you may be asked about this, but the phrase is glossed, so pass over it at this stage if you can.

8 **eam**: 'it', i.e. **urbem**, which is feminine. By now this should not cause difficulty.

10 **diūtius**: comparative adverb of **diū**. Bright students will see a connection between the words.

15 **audit**: 'listens to, obeys', a common meaning of this verb.

17–18 **amīcus cārus**: this is in apposition to Patroclus – 'Patroclus, his dear friend'; students may need help here: draw their attention to the commas.

20 **dēbēs mē ... mittere**: students may not recognize that **mē** is the object of **mittere**; they know that **dēbēs** requires an infinitive after it and if they falter tell them to look on to **mittere**.

21 **invītus**: 'unwilling', but English says 'unwillingly'; Latin uses the adjective since the word describes Achilles' state of mind, not the action of the verb.

24 **in eōs**: 'against them'; see note on line 2 above.

25 **fortissimus Trōiānōrum**: the phrase is in apposition to **Hector** (students will note commas).

Respondē Latīnē

1 Agamemnōn amīcōs ad Achillem mittit, quod ille nōn pugnat sed prope nāvēs manet ōtiōsus*.
2 amīcī Achillem iubent ad pugnam redīre et amīcōs iuvāre.
3 Patroclus dīcit: 'Achillēs, dēbēs amīcōs iuvāre. sī* tū nōn vīs* pugnāre, mitte mē in pugnam.'
4 Trōiānī territī sunt ubi vident arma Achillis.

* You will have to help them with these words, unless they remember them from the narrative.

Fābella: lūdus Flāviī

5 **salvē**: this is the imperative of the verb **salveō**, 'I am well'; the verb is only used in the imperative forms as an expression of greeting (plural: **salvēte**).
21 **scrībit**: **scrībō** can mean 'draw' as well as 'write'.
21, 27 **scrīpsit**: 'has written'; the context requires the perfect tense.

Grammar and exercises

The 3rd declension

Students should be warned that in the 3rd declension the nominative and accusative plural have the same form, which can result in ambiguity of meaning, e.g. **rēgēs prīncipēs vocant**. The subject of the verb usually comes before the object, so this probably means: 'The kings call the princes.' But the only sure guide is the sense demanded by the context. If students are reading intelligently, this ambiguity does not in practice cause difficulty.

3rd declension nouns with stems in **-i** decline exactly like other 3rd declension nouns except in the genitive plural (not yet learnt); in the other cases the **-i** has disappeared (a very few nouns retain **i**, e.g. **sitis** ('thirst'): acc. **siti-m**, gen. **siti-s**, dat. **sitī**, abl. **sitī**. Students do not need to know this.)

But they must note carefully that 3rd declension adjectives with stems in **-i** have ablative singular in **-ī**, not **-e**. (The fact is that languages do not develop in a perfectly logical way.)

This might be the time to show students the charts of nouns and adjectives in the Reference grammar (see note on chapter 3, p. 13 above).

You should make it clear that the gender of 3rd declension nouns must be carefully learnt in every vocabulary, since at present they have no way of telling from the nominative what the gender is; later some general rules on gender will be given.

Exercise 7.1

Students must be warned not to expect that adjective and noun always have identical endings, e.g. **magn-um puer-um**, **magn-am puell-am**, but **magn-am urb-em**, since adjective and noun belong to different declensions. The following exercise will entail a lot of thought, including consideration of gender.

Irregular verbs

We introduce **possum** and **eō**, two very common irregular verbs, early in the course since they are very useful in writing narratives. They present little difficulty when students have grasped that **possum** = **pot-sum** and that the stem of **eō** is **i**, not **e**; **e** only occurs in the forms **e-ō**, **e-unt** and the oblique cases of the present participle (**e-untem** etc.).

The infinitive of possum must be carefully learnt; compare **posse** to **esse**.

eō is most commonly found in compounds, which must be carefully learnt.

Background: Homer and the Iliad – 1

This background section is largely narrative in content and too much exploration would prove a distraction. However, a discussion which might prove helpful would deal with the nature of myth. What, if any, is the difference between a myth and a story (as in a novel)? A valuable attempt to grapple with this kind of distinction is that of C. S. Lewis: *An Experiment in Criticism*, Cambridge, ch. 5. It is important to establish that myths, however entertaining and trivial-seeming they may be on the surface, have a fundamental seriousness and truth. The lively story of the Judgement of Paris is one part of a mythological narrative which deals profoundly with the tragic nature of the world we live in.

It would be unwise to take the discussion of Homer any further than we have in our second paragraph.

Sources
The most amusing account of the Judgement of Paris – to which our own version owes something – is that of Lucian: *Deorum dialogi* 20. This has been entertainingly translated by Paul Turner in *Lucian: Satirical Sketches*, Penguin, pp. 55–64.

p. 48, para. 2: Why is Paris, a Trojan prince, tending flocks? The answer to this and to other such questions can be found in, e.g., P. Grimal: *Penguin Dictionary of Classical Mythology*, Penguin.

para. 3: The reference to Helen's face which 'launched a thousand ships' is to the scene in Christopher Marlowe's *Doctor Faustus* where Faustus addresses the phantom Helen of Troy:

Was this the face that launched a thousand ships,
And burnt the topless towers of Ilium?
Sweet Helen, make me immortal with a kiss…
I will be Paris, and for love of thee
Instead of Troy shall Wittenberg be sacked…

Illustrations

p. 45: the gateposts of the Lion Gate at Mycenae are 10$\frac{1}{2}$ feet high; on top of these is a massive lintel, 15 feet long, 6$\frac{1}{2}$ feet thick and 3$\frac{1}{4}$ feet high in the centre. A huge triangular slab of grey limestone (12 feet wide at the base, 10 feet high and 2 feet thick) shows a pillar supported by two lionesses which rest their feet on the altars that are the base of the column. Their heads are missing.
p. 46: this fine wall painting from Pompeii shows Achilles quarrelling with Agamemnon over the captive girl Briseis (on the right). Because of the intervention of Athena, goddess of wisdom, Achilles does not go through with his intention. (National Museum of Archaeology, Naples)
p. 47: this bust of Homer was often reproduced. The copy here is from the Louvre Museum, Paris.

Chapter 8

Cartoon captions

These introduce imperatives, singular and plural, of all conjugations. The cartoons should make the meaning clear, but students may need help over **nōlī**, **nōlīte**, which need to be followed by the infinitive.

Vocabulary

posse: you may need to comment on the irregular infinitive; compare **posse** (from **pot-sum**) to **esse** (from **sum**).

The death of Hector

2 **in Trōiānōs**: 'against the Trojans'.
5ff. For the appeals of Priam and Hecuba to their son, see *Iliad* 22.25–89.
10, 27 **nōn audit**: 'does not listen to', 'pays no attention to'.
10ff. Hector knows that he will be killed by Achilles if he stands fast but he is constrained by his sense of honour not to run away (*Iliad* 22.199ff.) until Achilles draws near and he panics (135ff.).
17 **resistit**: the verb here has its basic meaning of 'stands firm' rather than the commoner meaning 'resists'.

sē vertit: 'he turns himself' = 'he turns'; **vertere** is a transitive verb and so here requires the reflexive pronoun **sē** as object (see chapter 14).
20 **parmam**: we use **parma** for 'shield' – certainly not the right word; it is a small, round wicker shield, but **scūtum**, which is nearer to the Homeric tower shield, is neuter, which would present grammatical difficulty.
22 **summā vī**: **vīs** ('might') has the irregular ablative **vī**. **summus** ('highest') is often used to mean 'greatest'. The phrase is glossed and comment is probably unnecessary.
24 **facinus**: if you are asked about an accusative ending in **-us**, you will have to explain that it is the accusative of a 3rd declension neuter noun (neuter nouns and adjectives are dealt with in chapter 10).

The ransom of Hector

In mutilating Hector's body and not allowing its burial, Achilles in his anger exceeds all accepted norms of behaviour. The gods decide that he must return the body to Troy for burial, and they send Iris to inspire Priam to go to Achilles and beg him to return his son's body. When Priam enters Achilles' tent and falls at his knees and kisses his hands (*Iliad* 24.477ff.), Achilles remembers his own old father; his anger drops from him at last and he receives Priam kindly and releases Hector's body. The *Iliad* begins with the words 'the wrath of Achilles'; in the final scene this anger is assuaged.

1–2 This sentence with **diū** in emphatic position repeated three times (*anaphora*) and absence of connecting particle between each part (*asyndeton*) is characteristic of Latin of emotional or elevated style.

3 deus Mercurius: On Mercury (Greek Hermes), see the note on chapter 12, Infelix Dido, line 12 below.

8 Achillēs, ubi…: note the word order; Latin puts the subject of the main verb before the conjunction which introduces a subordinate clause; English does not usually do this.

Question 5 is open-ended; its answer requires more than a literal understanding of the Latin; it is the first step towards a critical understanding of literature.

Grammar and exercises

Imperatives

Imperatives have already occurred in the narratives; they are easy to learn and cause little trouble.

nōlī, **nōlīte**: these forms are the imperatives of **nōlō**, 'I am unwilling'; **nōlīte abīre** is literally 'be unwilling to go away', i.e. 'don't go away'.

Exercise 8.2

Remind your students that English uses the same imperative form for singular and plural but Latin has two forms according to whether one or more persons are being addressed.

Prepositions

These need frequent revision.

Compound verbs

Once the principle of forming compound verbs from simple is understood, students' vocabulary is considerably extended with no extra effort of memory. We do not consider it necessary to gloss every new compound verb which occurs in the narratives. Some changes of spelling occur in the formation of compounds for the sake of euphony, e.g. **in** become **im-** before a followimg **m**; **ad** becomes **ac-** before a following **c**. These changes need not be learnt; once encountered, they become obvious.

-que

Students may find the use of **-que** difficult at first. **-que** denotes a closer connection than **et**. It is never attached to a final **-e** or **c**.

In exercise 8.6 students will need help as to when they should use **et** and when **-que**; **cum mātreque** or **labōrāreque**, for example, would not be correct. Either warn them to use **et** except in 1 and 3; or tell them they need not use **-que** at all.

Background: The Iliad – 2

The story is taken from *Iliad* 24. This is one of the greatest and most intense episodes in Western literature and defies adequate summary and commentary in a beginners' language course. Yet we hope that even in this skeletal form it will convey at least some of Homer's power.

Some possible themes for exploration:

The treatment of the dead was a matter of enormous importance in the ancient world. The story of Sophocles' *Antigone* gives a striking illustration of this, and suggests that many Greeks would have disapproved of pushing one's hatred of one's enemies beyond death. How do your pupils feel about Achilles' behaviour to the dead Hector (p. 52, paras 1–2)?

In the modern world too the treatment of the dead seems a matter of profound significance. When a ship or oil rig sinks, there is intense pressure from the families of the victims to recover their bodies. It seems that they cannot come to terms with their loss until their loved ones have been duly laid to rest. This is deeply relevant to a poem that ends with the funeral of Hector (p. 53, para. 4).

The poignancy of the meeting between the king of Troy and the Greek hero who has killed so many of his sons should be stressed.

In p. 53, para. 3, first the theme of the love between fathers and sons should be noted. This is the emotion which unites Achilles and Priam as they weep together. Then your pupils should be asked whether they feel that Achilles made the right choice.

In the final paragraph, the insubstantial shadow of existence in the Underworld should be stressed. When the ghost of Achilles speaks to Odysseus there, he says that he would rather be the humblest man on earth than king of all the dead (*Odyssey* 11.488–91).

p. 53, para. 5: Achilles' heel: Achilles' mother dipped him as a child in the waters of the Styx to make him invulnerable. His heel, which she was holding him by, escaped the treatment.

Illustrations

p. 50: on the neck of this red-figure vase of about 490–480 BC by the Berlin Painter, Achilles (on the left) and

Hector (on the right) carry the arms of Greek hoplites of the fifth century BC, not of Homeric warriors; and neither hoplites nor Homeric warriors would have fought naked. As Achilles moves in for the kill, the already-wounded Hector appears to have given up the struggle and exposes his body to death. The contrasting angling of the spears and positioning of the shields are deeply poignant. (British Museum, London)

p. 51: this mosaic of the third century AD shows Achilles dragging Hector's body round the walls of Troy. (Vatican Museums, Rome)

p. 53: this Attic red-figure cup of about 490–480 BC gives a rather different story of the ransom of Hector from that of Homer. To the left Priam, with attendants carrying Hector's ransom (one of them just visible), approaches an arrogant Achilles who reclines on a couch above Hector's body. The danger latent in Achilles is shown by the hanging armour and the dagger he holds. In Homer's version Achilles takes great care that Priam and he should not be together with Hector's corpse. He feels this would arouse emotions dangerously. (Kunsthistorisches Museum, Vienna)

Chapter 9

Cartoon captions

The meaning of these captions is evident from the pictures, but careful students will be worried by the forms **puellae** and **puerī**, which they have learnt as nominative plurals. You will have to warn them that the meaning of these forms is ambiguous in isolation, but add that the context will make make it clear whether they are genitive singular, meaning 'of', or nominative plural. E.g. caption 1: '**puer**, nom. sing., must be the subject. The verb is singular and so **puellae** cannot be the subject.'

You must make sure your students understand the punctuation: the girl's = of the girl; the girls' = of the girls.

The fall of Troy

The passage is broadly based on *Aeneid* 2, not the *Iliad* which ends with the funeral of Hector. The *Aeneid* begins abruptly with Aeneas and his followers sailing from Sicily on the last lap of their journey from Troy to Italy, but they are overwhelmed by a storm which drives them to Libya; there they are received hospitably by Queen Dido, who is building the city of Carthage; she entertains Aeneas and his followers at a great banquet after which she asks Aeneas to tell the story of the fall of Troy. The story of the fall of Troy and their subsequent wanderings is thus a flash-back, occupying Books 2 and 3 of the poem.

1 **decem annōs**: see note on chapter 7, line 7 above. The phrase is again glossed. You could now, if you like, contrast this phrase in the accusative with with **prīmā lūce** (line 14), where the ablative expresses 'time when', making the point that expressions of time are regularly without a preposition.

6 **domumne**: students may fail to recognize the interrogative affix **-ne** (see chapter 6).

9 **attentē**: not glossed; students should recognize the adverbial form and guess from the context ('attentively' etc.).

17 **stantem**: accusative of present participle of **stō**. In Part I we treat present participles as ordinary adjectives (always glossed) and as such they present no difficulty.

18 **equō nōlīte crēdere**: students may ask about the case of **equō**; if so, you will have to say that some verbs, including **crēdō**, take the dative, which they have not yet met.

Compare *Aeneid* 2.48–9, where Laocoon warns the Trojans not to take the horse into the city:

> equō nē crēdite, Teucrī.
> quidquid id est, timeō Danaōs et dōna ferentēs.

Don't trust the horse, Trojans. Whatever it is, I fear the Greeks even when they bring (bringing) gifts.

Brighter students might like to hear these famous lines, and with some help understand them.

20 **laetī**: the adjective may be translated by an adverb, 'joyfully' (compare note on **invītus** in chapter 7, line 21).

21 **epulās**: epulae is plural in form but singular in meaning (compare **nūndinae**, 'market day').

22 **quī**: 'who'; in Part I we use the relative pronoun in the nominative freely; it is glossed and presents no difficulty.

30 **urbem dēlent**: excavations at Troy show that Troy VIIa, Priam's Troy, was in fact sacked and burnt.

Respondē Latīnē

1 Graecī quī in īnsulā sunt nāvēs cōnscendunt et ad urbem redeunt.
2 Graecī quī in equō cēlātī* sunt tacitī exeunt et vigilēs occīdunt.
3 vigilēs* Trōiānōrum ēbriī* sunt; dormiunt.

* These words have not been learnt.

Answers to the questions require students to use the relative pronoun **quī**; they may need some help here, but no elaborate explanation is necessary, since the nominative masculine plural **qu-ī** has the same ending as that of **colōn-ī** etc.

Aenēās ex urbe Trōiā fugit

This story is told at greater length in chapter 11, when

Aeneas recounts his adventures to Dido.

5 nōs Trōiānī: 'we Trojans'; both words form the subject of **supersumus**, which may occasion difficulty.

6 novam Trōiam: the task of founding a new Troy is imposed on Aeneas by the dead Hector, who appears to him in a dream while Troy is burning (see chapter 11). From then on Aeneas is the man of destiny; he will found a new Troy and from it ultimately will spring Rome.

9 diū: in fact it took Aeneas and his followers seven years to reach Italy, just as it took Odysseus ten to get back to Ithaca.

Grammar and exercises

The genitive case

Possessive and *partitive* genitives are both used in these exercises: possessive, e.g. **colōnī ager**, 'the field of (= belonging to) the farmer'; partitive, e.g. **multī colōnōrum**, 'many of the farmers'; **fortissimus omnium hērōum**, 'the bravest of all the heroes'. Since both are rendered 'of' in English, the distinction is not important at present.

The partitive genitive is also used after adverbs implying quantity, e.g. **satis cibī**, 'enough (of) food'; and after pronouns, e.g. **quid novī?**, 'what (of) news?' (see Part II, chapter 24).

Note that in the 1st and 2nd declensions, the genitive singular and the nominative plural have the same form; this can result in ambiguity of meaning, e.g.

puerī colōnī agrum intrant.

The boys enter the farmer's field.

This could, as far as case endings go, mean 'The farmers enter the boy's field', but word order and context will make the meaning clear; the sense demanded by the context is the safer guide, since word order is flexible.

You may have to remind students of the rules of English punctuation, viz. boy's = of the boy; boys' = of the boys.

Adverbs

Since adverbs are here officially introduced, you may need to clear up the following points:

1 adverbs usually modify verbs, e.g. **celeriter ambulāmus**, 'we are walking quickly'; **celeriter** tells you how we are walking. But some may also modify adjectives, e.g. **valdē fessus est**, 'he is extremely tired'.

2 English sometimes uses adverbs where an adjective is more logically correct, e.g. Horatia returns home happily, but Latin says: **Horātia laeta domum redit**, since **laeta** describes Horatia, not the way in which she returns. So also **invītus discēdit**, 'he departs unwilling(ly)'.

Background: Virgil and the Aeneid

In this chapter we leave the *Iliad* and move on to Virgil. Aeneas is an important though comparatively minor character in the *Iliad*. (Teachers may find it helpful to use the excellent index of M. Hammond's translation of the *Iliad* (Penguin) to see the role played by Aeneas in that poem.) He is of course the leading figure in Virgil's *Aeneid*, Book 2 of which is summarized in the present chapter. The way in which the worlds of Homer and Virgil interrelate is dealt with in the background section of chapter 10.

Through the figure of Aeneas, Virgil articulates the fundamental theme of his poem, the struggle between *pietās* (a sense of duty to family and nation) and *fūror* (uncontrolled frenzy). The former is a constructive and positive force, the latter a profoundly destructive one.

Amid the Greeks' sack of Troy, Aeneas finds himself possessed by *fūror* (p. 59, para. 2). Hector's orders to preserve the Trojan gods and to found a new city (p. 59, para. 1) fly from his mind. He assumes that he will be killed and wants to take as many Greeks as possible to the Underworld with him. He becomes in effect an emblem of *fūror*.

His mother Venus convinces him through an apocalyptic vision (*Aeneid* 2.604–18) that Troy is finished and that his duty is to the future (p. 59, para. 3). As he leaves the city with father, son and household gods, he is transformed into an emblem of *pietās*. In fact the image of Aeneas supporting his father on his shoulders and holding his son by the hand was mass-produced in the Roman world. It could be picked up in any souvenir shop. Thanks to Virgil, *pietās* became big business.

It is important that you convey something of the meaning of *pietās* and *fūror* to your pupils. Question 2 may make it clear whether you have succeeded since the best answers are likely to mention *fūror* to balance its opposite.

In a manner altogether characteristic of Virgil, the story continues tragically with Aeneas' loss of his wife (p. 59, para. 4). This is an episode of enormous pathos, especially the moment of the thrice-frustrated embrace. In Virgil's poem *pietās* is never distant from tragedy. Question 1: after your pupils have dealt with this question, you might read them Menelaus' account of Helen's behaviour on this night (*Odyssey* 4.266–89).

Two excellent guides to the main themes of the *Aeneid* are W. Camps: *An Introduction to the Aeneid*, Oxford, and R. D. Williams: *Aeneas and the Roman Hero*, Macmillan, repr. Bristol Classical Press. D. West has translated the poem admirably for Penguin.

Illustrations

p. 55: the walls of Troy in north-west Turkey. They

were excavated by Heinrich Schliemann in the late nineteenth century. These are the sturdy Mycenaean walls of Troy VI and in *Iliad* 16 Homer refers to their most unusual feature, the offsets which divide the wall into different sections.

p. 56: part of a relief on a funerary urn of about 670 BC. The horse is mounted on wheels. The Greek warriors are clearly visible, some of them even holding their armour out of the apertures! (Mykonos Museum)

p. 57: on this vase by the Cleophrades Painter from the first quarter of the fifth century BC, Priam, as he sits on the altar, 'holds his hands to his head in a touching gesture of despair. His head has been cut and is bleeding; the battered and gashed body of his grandson lies sprawled in his lap. A beautiful young warrior puts his hand on the old king's shoulder, not to comfort him, but to steady him before brutally delivering the fatal blow' (Susan Woodford, *An Introduction to Greek Art*, Duckworth, p. 72). (National Museum of Archaeology, Naples)

p. 58: a Roman mosaic of the early third century AD showing Virgil with the Muses Clio (Muse of History) or Calliope (Epic poetry) on the left, and Melpomene (Tragedy) on the right. (Bardo Museum, Tunis)

p. 59: Gian Lorenzo Bernini was only fifteen when he sculpted this marble group jointly with his father in 1613. It shows Aeneas as he escapes from Troy, carrying his father Anchises and leading his son Ascanius by the hand. Anchises carries an image of the goddess Vesta. Ascanius holds the sacred fire, and Aeneas wears a lion skin. This was a highly popular subject in the ancient world. (Galleria Borghese, Rome)

Chapter 10

Cartoon captions

Neuter nouns of the 2nd and 3rd declensions are introduced in these captions; these could only cause difficulty in the forms **lītus** (caption 1), which will look to your students like a 2nd declension nominative singular, and **saxa** (captions 2 and 4), which will look like a 1st declension nominative singular. Students may be guided by the sense to understand these forms correctly; if not you will have to comment briefly.

Polyphēmus

We recommend that the story of Odysseus and the Cyclops in the background section of this chapter should be read before starting this passage. The passage itself is broadly based on *Aeneid* 3.570–680.

2 **ubi**: 'where'; the word is used both as a relative adverb, as here, and as an interrogative 'where?'. (The **ubi** clause expresses purpose and correct Latin would

demand the subjunctive **possint**, 'where they might found . . .'.)

3 **multōs labōrēs**, **multa perīcula**: this shape of phrase with repeated adjective and absence of connection (asyndeton) is characteristic of Latin; English would probably join the phrases by 'and'.

　labōrēs: 'sufferings'; this meaning is common in poetry.

6 **Scylla**: Scylla was a sea-monster who lived in a cave opposite the whirlpool Charybdis on the straits of Messina between Sicily and Italy. She had six heads and six arms; when Odysseus in trying to avoid Charybdis steered too near to Scylla, she snatched his best six men from his ship and swallowed them down, while they stretched out their arms to him in despair (*Odyssey* 12.234–58). Later, when Odysseus' ship was sunk by a storm and he alone survived by clinging to the mast, he was sucked down into the whirlpool of Charybdis and only just survived (*Odyssey* 12.426–46). The adventures of Odysseus and Aeneas overlap both here and in the story of the Cyclops.

8 **Anchīsēs**: Aeneas has relied on the wisdom of his father Anchises ever since they left Troy. Anchises died in Sicily soon after their escape from Polyphemus, leaving Aeneas to battle on alone.

11 **montem Aetnam**: Etna is Europe's highest volcano (10,758 ft) and was intermittently active in ancient times, as it still is now; in the 470s BC there was a spectacular eruption which inspired Pindar to write of it:

> Pure founts of unapproachable fire
> Belch from its depths.
> In the day-time its rivers
> Pour forth a glowing stream of smoke:
> But in the darkness red flame rolls
> And into the deep level sea
> Throws the rocks roaring.
> 　　(Pythian 1.21ff.)

Virgil pictures Etna in eruption when the Trojans land there:

> . . . nearby, Aetna thunderously erupts.
> Ever and anon it discharges at heaven a mirky cloud,
> A swirl of pitch-black smoke lurid with white-hot cinders,
> And volleys huge balls of flame, singeing the very stars.
> Ever and anon, as if the mountain's guts were being coughed up,
> It belches rock, and groaning, vomits out thick streams
> Of lava, seething up from its roots.
> 　　(Aeneid 3.571–7, trans. Cecil Day Lewis)

16 **hominem**: the unhappy Greek, who had been forgotten by Ulysses when he escaped from Polyphemus' cave, threw himself on the mercy of the

Trojans and was offered protection by Anchises. He gave a harrowing account of his sufferings and warned the Trojans of the danger from the Cyclopes (*Aeneid* 3.590–654).

18 fūgērunt: the context demands a perfect tense; it is glossed and need not delay you.

19 hīc: 'here'. The adverb **hīc** is distinguished from the pronoun **hic** by the long **ī**.

20 Cyclōpibus: the dative is introduced in the next chapter. You might, if students ask about **Cyclōpibus**, give them a brief preview of the dative as indirect object.

26ff. The Cyclopes had only one eye in the middle of their foreheads. Odysseus had blinded Polyphemus by driving a burning stake into his eye. Virgil's description of Polyphemus is at once terrifying and touched with sympathy for the blind monster (the Greek survivor has just warned the Trojans of the danger they are in):

> vix ea fātus erat summō cum monte vidēmus
> ipsum inter pecudēs vastā se mōle moventem
> pāstōrem Polyphēmum et lītora nōta petentem,
> mōnstrum horrendum, īnfōrme, ingēns, cui lūmen
>   adēmptum.
> trunca manum pīnūs regit et vestīgia firmat:
> lānigerae comitantur ovēs; ea sōla voluptās
> sōlāmenque malī.

Scarcely had he said this when we see on the top of the mountain the shepherd Polyphemus himself moving his vast bulk and making for the shores he knew, a horrifying monster, ugly, huge, robbed of his eye. The trunk of a pine tree guides his hand and supports his steps; his woolly sheep accompany him; they are his only pleasure and the comfort of his distress.

(*Aeneid* 3.655–61)

Fābella: Aeneas escapes from Polyphemus

In the latter part of this playlet we depart shamelessly from both the letter and the spirit of Virgil. In the *Aeneid* (3.679) Polyphemus hears the Trojans departing, tries to catch them and, when he cannot, raises a tremendous shout which summons the other Cyclopes. They reach the shore too late; the Trojans are already out of their range. In the *Odyssey* Polyphemus hurls huge rocks at the Trojan ships which first wash them back to shore and then out to sea; Odysseus mocks Polyphemus, exulting in the success of his stratagem. Aeneas was far too austere and anxious a character to behave like this; in the earlier part of the *Aeneid* he is a sad, bewildered figure, struggling to fulfil a destiny imposed on him by the gods, often despairing, sometimes failing in his duty.

7 ecce!: 'look!'; the word has occurred three times and is not glossed.

18 puerīlibus: not glossed – to be guessed from the context.

19 dī immortālēs: 'immortal gods!' **deus** has two forms of nominative plural: **deī** or **dī**.

fābulōsus: from **fābula**, and thus to be guessed; but students are likely to be misled by modern usage (e.g. 'we had a fabulous time'). Would they understand correctly 'a fabulous monster'?

26 virum: genitive plural, for which **vir** has two forms, **virōrum** or **virum**.

Grammar and exercises

Neuter nouns and adjectives
Students will notice that neuter nom., voc. and acc. have the same form and that in the plural these cases end **-a** in all declensions. The genitive, dative and ablative endings are the same as those of masculine nouns in the 2nd declension, and in the 3rd the same as those of other nouns.

But they should note carefully that 3rd declension adjectives with stems in **-i** have ablative singular in **-ī** (e.g. **omnī**), and keep **-i** throughout the neuter plural, e.g. **omni-a**, **omni-um**, **omni-bus**.

There are very few 3rd declension adjectives with stems in consonants and only one occurs in Part I (**pauper**, chapter 15).

Exercise 10.1
This important exercise will take considerable thought and care; students may be inclined to give the same ending to adjective and noun. It might be best to do the first few examples orally.

Background: The Aeneid – 2

The contrasts between the world of Homer and that of Virgil offer opportunities for discussion. In the figure of Aeneas Virgil is forging a different type of hero from the Homeric models. While possessed of the stature and charisma of the latter, the prototype Roman leader is burdened by his sense of responsibility, his *pietās*. Homer's heroes are essentially concerned with themselves. Your pupils can discuss which they would rather be, Odysseus or Aeneas.

The books referred to at the end of the last chapter's teacher's notes will again prove valuable here.

Odysseus and the Cyclops
This section, based on *Odyssey* 9, should have been read before the Latin story in our chapter. Here the focus of discussion could be upon the contrast between man at a primitive stage of development (the Cyclops) and the technologically and verbally inventive Odysseus.

The characters in the *Odyssey* are often defined by their attitudes to the Homeric conventions of hospitality.

On a guest's arrival, a host was expected to give him a meal. Only after that meal could he ask his guest's name; and later, gifts of hospitality would be exchanged. Your pupils could discuss the ways in which these conventions are perverted in the Cyclops episode.

The Greek plural of **Cyclōps** is **Cyclōpes**.

Question 2: this episode is a particularly rewarding one in the way it brings out Odysseus' personality, celebrating his lively inventiveness and his jubilant courage but on two occasions revealing him as a far from responsible leader.

Homer's telling of the story of the Cyclops is, of course, inimitable. If you have a translation of the *Odyssey* available (especially the revised E. V. Rieu in Penguin), you might read from Book 9 – as well as from 12 if you wish to develop the references to Scylla and Charybdis in para. 2 of the Latin story.

Illustrations

p. 62: Mount Etna in Sicily is here shown erupting in 1971. For more information about the volcano, see the commentary on the Latin above.

p. 63: this Hellenistic head of the Cyclops from the first century BC shows his single eye between the two eye sockets. (Museum of Fine Arts, Boston)

p. 65: this Romano-African mosaic from the fourth century AD shows Odysseus offering a bowl of wine to the Cyclops in his cave. An eviscerated sheep lies over the Cyclops' knee. (Villa Imperiale, Piazza Armerina, Sicily)

p. 66 (top): this lively representation of Odysseus blinding the Cyclops is from an Attic black-figure vase of 530–510 BC. (British Museum, London)

p. 66 (bottom): this vase of about 510 BC by the Sappho Painter shows the armed Odysseus under a ram. (Badisches Landesmuseum, Karlsruhe)

Chapter 11

This and the following chapter are based on *Aeneid* Book 1, in which Aeneas is wrecked in Libya and meets Dido; Books 2 and 3, in which he tells the story of the fall of Troy and his subsequent wanderings; and Book 4, in which Virgil tells of the love of Dido and Aeneas and Dido's death.

Cartoon captions

The cartoons should succeed in making the meaning of the captions apparent. But the forms of the dative are identical with those of other cases: 1st declension, **puellae** in isolation could be genitive singular, dative singular or nominative plural, **puellīs** could be dative or ablative plural; 2nd declension, **puerō** could be dative or ablative singular, **puerīs** dative or ablative plural. The context is the only safe guide and as your students are used to reading whole sentences, they may not be much troubled by this. If possible, leave comment until you come to study the grammar.

The meeting of Dido and Aeneas

1 **tempestās**: the storm is caused by Juno, who is the enemy of Troy and wishes to prevent Aeneas and the Trojan survivors from reaching Italy. She goes to Aeolus, king of the winds, and orders him to loose all the winds (see *Aeneid* 1.51ff.).

7 **mihi prōpositum est**: 'it is the intention for me'; this use of the dative is explained in the Grammar; as the phrase is glossed, there is no need to delay over it here.

8 **ūnō cum amīcō**: it is time students became familiar with this word order; it will probably need no comment.

10 **ō fortūnātī**: cf. *Aeneid* 1.437: 'ō fortūnātī, quōrum iam moenia surgunt.'

22 **pepulit**: the context demands the use of the perfect.

29–30 **īnfandum, rēgīna, iubēs renovāre dolōrem**: taken directly from *Aeneid* 2.3. Students may need prompting to see that **īnfandum** agrees with **dolōrem**.

Respondē Latīnē

1 Dīdō ad templum accēdit cum multīs prīncipibus.

2 Dīdō Aenēam benignē accipit, quod fāma Trōiānōrum eī nōta est.

3 Dīdō Aenēam iubet omnēs labōrēs Trōiānōrum nārrāre.

Aeneas tells of the fall of Troy

This comprehension passage is rather long, but the first paragraph repeats the sense of what they read in chapter 9, so it should be easy. You may wish to do the first two paragraphs orally.

9 **fuge, Aenēā…**: compare:

> 'heu fuge, nāte deā, tēque hīs' ait 'ēripe flammīs.
> hostis habet mūrōs; ruit altō ā culmine Trōia …'
>
> 'Alas! flee, goddess-born,' he said, 'and save yourself from these flames. The enemy holds the walls; Troy collapses from its high citadel.'
> (*Aeneid* 2.289–90)

Your students could understand these lines given **nāte deā** = 'goddess born' (Aeneas' mother was the goddess Venus) and **culmine** = 'top'.

11 **sacra**: Virgil says (Hector speaking):

> sacra suōsque tibī commendat Trōia penātēs;
> hōs cape fātōrum comitēs.
>
> Troy entrusts to you her *sacred emblems* and her

guardian gods; take these as companions to your destiny.

(*Aeneid* 2.293–4)

The **penātēs** were the guardian spirits of the household or, in this case, of the city.

Hector then brings Aeneas the sacred ribbons, Vesta (goddess of the hearth) and the eternal fire, which signifies the continuing life of the city; this fire was tended by the Vestal Virgins throughout the history of Rome. By entrusting the **sacra** of Troy to Aeneas in this dream, Hector imposes on him a sacred mission, to guard the life of Troy. Almost the first words Aeneas speaks in the whole *Aeneid* are addressed to his mother Venus, who meets him in Libya disguised as a Carthaginian girl:

sum pius Aenēās, raptōs quī ex hoste penātēs classe vehō mēcum.

I am pious Aeneas, who rescued the city gods from the enemy and carry them in my fleet.

(*Aeneid* 1.378–9)

pius is repeatedly used by Virgil to describe Aeneas; the concept of **pietās** includes the duty owed to the gods, to one's country and to one's family.

13 **arma capiō**: cf. *Aeneid* 2.314:

arma āmēns capiō; nec sat ratiōnis in armīs.

In madness I seized my arms; nor had I any rational plan in taking up arms.

It was mad to try to carry on the fight after Hector's warning; Aeneas gave way to **fūror** and **īra**.

17 **imāgō**: Aeneas' attempt to carry on the fight led him to Priam's palace; there he saw the old king murdered by the son of Achilles. It was this sight which brought to his mind a picture (**imāgō**) of his own father whom he had deserted.

Grammar and exercises

The dative case: indirect object
The concept of the indirect object presents little difficulty except for the ambiguity of English in sentences such as 'Scintilla tells her daughter a story', where 'her daughter' looks superficially like the direct object.

The dative singular of the 1st declension is the same in form as that of the genitive singular and nominative plural. This may result in ambiguity of meaning but usually the context will make the meaning clear.

Exercise 11.2
This exercise is intended to help students to recognize indirect objects that are disguised in English; as it is rather cumbersome it may be best done orally.

Exercise 11.3
You may need to ask your students to analyse the sentences before translating them into Latin, e.g.
'The father gives his son the food.'
Verb: gives
Subject: the father (Who gives the food?)
Object: the food (What does he give?)
Indirect object: (to) his son (To whom does he give it?)

Further uses of the dative case
1 Verbs taking the dative occasion little difficulty, once students understand that these are indirect objects; most dative verbs are intransitive in Latin, though they appear transitive in English, e.g. 'I resist' in English is transitive; **resistō** is intransitive, since it properly means 'I stand up to'.

Some 'dative' verbs can take both a direct and an indirect object, e.g. **hoc tibi imperō**, 'I order this to you', i.e. 'I give you this order'; **hoc tibi persuādeō**, 'I persuade this to you', i.e. 'I persuade you of this'. But students do not need to know this yet.

2 The 'dative of the person concerned' is the heading we use to cover what the grammarians call the 'dative of advantage', 'the dative of disadvantage' and 'the dative of possession'. This is a harder concept for students to understand. There is little difficulty in sentences such as **hoc tibi facimus**, 'we are doing this *for you*', but Latin often uses such datives where English uses a possessive adjective, e.g.

mihi nōmen est Mārcus. The name for me is Marcus. = My name is Marcus.

mihi est prōpositum. It is the intention for me. = It is my intention.

est mihi equus. There is a horse for me. = I have a horse (dative of possession).

English and Latin idiom differ. This may become an increasing problem, and it is here that literal-minded students may falter. They must be encouraged to be flexible in their understanding, grasping whole sense units together, not translating word by word. Those brought up on an inductive reading approach will encounter less difficulty here than those taught on traditional methods.

Exercise 11.4
2 **eīs imperat ... facere**: **imperō** + infinitive is used in classical Latin, though less often than the **ut/nē** construction of indirect command (**iubeō** and **vetō** are always used with the infinitive).

Background: Dido, queen of Carthage

The three questions are the obvious areas for discussion in this summary of the Dido material from Book 1 of the *Aeneid*. Pygmalion's *fūror* in p. 71, para. 1 could be emphasized as could Dido's leadership qualities in paras 3, 4 and 5. The theme of city building could be stressed (para. 5). It is an important one in a poem which looks forward to the building of the walls of lofty Rome (*Aeneid* 1.7). In contrast to this theme, Aeneas is in Book 2 to tell Dido the story of the fall of Troy.

Sources

p. 71, para. 3: Dido's leadership qualities are summed up at *Aeneid* 1.364 in the words **dux fēmina factī**, 'it was a woman who took the lead in the action'.

para. 5: 'ō fortūnātī...': *Aeneid* 1.437; cf. line 10 of 'The meeting of Dido and Aeneas'.

Illustrations

p. 68: this beautiful miniature from a fifteenth-century manuscript of the works of Virgil shows (starting at the bottom): Aeneas (in blue) arriving at the coast of North Africa; he meets his mother Venus who, in her disguise as a huntress (note the bow, arrows and dogs), tells him Dido's story; Troy being built; Dido and Aeneas presiding at a banquet. At the top left, Aeneas' companions, who had been thought lost in a storm, arrive safely and are welcomed by Dido. The words below are those of the first line of the *Aeneid*: 'arma virumque canō, Trōiae quī prīmus ab ōrīs' (I sing of arms and the man who was the first from the shores of Troy (to reach Italy)). (Edinburgh University Library)

p. 70: a book from the fifth century AD shows fighting at Troy. (Bibliotheca Ambrosiana, Milan)

p. 72: this illustration from a fourth-century manuscript of Virgil shows Aeneas and his companion Achates gazing in wonder from the top of a hill at the building of Carthage. The wheel – the painting is damaged – is part of a crane. (Vatican Museums, Rome)

Chapter 12

This is a review chapter, which introduces no new grammar, but the Latin is rather harder than that of earlier chapters, especially at the end, where we have kept as close as possible to Virgil's words. Students may well need quite a lot of help. Our narrative is more inadequate than usual to convey the power of Virgil's poetry; you may wish to read some of *Aeneid* Book 4 to your students in translation.

Caption

gladium, **pectus**, **trānsfīgit** are all unknown; the picture will probably guide students to their meaning and they are glossed when they occur in the narrative.

Īnfēlīx Dīdō

Īnfēlīx: 'ill-starred'; the word is first used to describe Dido at the end of Book 1 (749) as she listens to Aeneas and begins to fall in love with him. This love will lead to her death.

1 **dīcendī**: if students ask about this form, you could say that it is the genitive of a verbal noun formed from **dīcō**; gerunds are explained in Part III.

5–6 **eīs placet**: 'it pleases them', i.e. 'they decide'. This is the first occurrence of an impersonal verb; it should not occasion difficulty and is better not explained yet.

12 **Mercurī**: vocative of Mercurius; compare **fīlī**, vocative of **fīlius**. Mercury (Greek Hermes) was the messenger of the gods, the bringer of good luck and gain, and a guide to men. He wore winged sandals of gold; cf. *Aeneid* 4.239–41: 'He binds his winged sandals on his feet, which carry him aloft on wings over the seas and over the land along with the rushing wind.'

25 **moritūram**: literally 'about to die' (future participle); Aeneas is warned what will happen if he deserts Dido.

28 **sponte**: this word, the ablative of a noun of which the nominative would be **spōns**, occurs only in the form **sponte** (and very occasionally **spontis**), usually with the adjectives **meā**, **tuā**, **suā** attached, meaning 'of one's free will', e.g. **hoc fēcit suā sponte**, 'he did this on his own volition'. Virgil makes Aeneas end his lame defence to Dido: 'Italiam nōn sponte sequor' (*Aeneid* 4.361).

30 **tē manet**: **maneō** ('I stay, wait') can be used transitively, 'I await'.

sērius ōcius: literally 'later, more swiftly'. The two comparative adverbs are placed in asyndeton; English must connect them by 'or' (the idiom is not here used by Virgil but occurs several times in Horace, e.g. *Odes* 2.3.26).

ultiōnem: remind your students that Dido's prophecy of vengeance was fulfilled a thousand years later when Hannibal invaded Italy in 218 BC.

Mors Dīdōnis

This jejune account of Dido's death is quite inadequate to represent the splendour of Virgil's account; we strongly recommend you to read to your students a translation of *Aeneid* 4.631–705.

6 **gladium**: the sword she took was a gift from Aeneas.

7 **pectus trānsfīgit**: her death was slow and painful; she was released from her sufferings by Juno, who sent Iris to despatch her to the Underworld.

11 **fūmum**: as Aeneas sails towards Italy, he looks back; seeing the smoke rising from Dido's pyre, he guesses the reason for it (*Aeneid* 5.4–8).

Fābella: Aenēās Dīdōnem dēserit

This is by far the longest playlet and you may not have time for it; but it could be done quite quickly, if you ask your students to prepare it out of class. It falls into four miniature scenes, of which the second, third and fourth are based on Virgil; the first, the strike of the Carthaginian workmen, is a comic interlude to relieve the gloom of this chapter; if it seems in doubtful taste, we appeal to the precedents set by Shakespeare (e.g. the porter scene in *Macbeth*).

17 **Iovis**: **Iuppiter** declines: **Iovem, Iovis, Iovī, Iove**.

20 **an**: this particle is used in double questions, e.g. **utrum deus es an homō?**, 'Are you a god or a man?'

26 **tibi īrātus est**: **īrātus** is the perfect participle of the deponent verb **īrāscor** which takes the dative. In the note on dative verbs (grammar section of chapter 11), we warned students that **īrātus** is found with the dative case.

29 **Trōiānīs**: 'for the Trojans'; a good example of the 'dative of the person concerned' – students may need reminding of this usage.

Grammar and exercises

No new grammar is introduced in this chapter.

Review of nouns and adjectives
It is now time for students to consolidate thoroughly their knowledge of nouns and adjectives of the first three declensions. They should study the charts of the first three declensions in the Reference grammar (pp. 145–6). These tables include 3rd declension adjectives with consonant stems; though some are common, the only one occurring in Part I is **pauper** in chapter 15. This could be omitted for the time being, although its declension presents no difficulty; if you ask students to learn it, warn them that it declines like 3rd declension nouns with consonant stems, i.e. abl. sing. **-e**, not **-ī**, gen. pl. **-um**, not **-ium**, neuter pl. nom., voc. and acc. **-a**, not **-ia**.

In listing the uses of the cases, we give the meanings of the ablative in the traditional summary – 'by, with or from'. We have so far glossed ablative phrases, apart from ablatives occurring after prepositions. The uses of the ablative are extensive and complex and we do not explain them until Part II, chapter 22. We continue to gloss many occurrences of the ablative without prepositions but students may be expected to recognize simple uses such as **magnā vōce clāmat**, 'he shouts with/in a loud voice'. It will help students at this stage to be familiar with the traditional rubric 'by, with or from', inadequate as this is.

'est' and 'sunt'
The existential use of **esse**, i.e. when **esse** is not a copula joining subject and complement but means 'exists', is not particularly common but needs to be known.

Background: From Aeneas to Romulus

'Romulus and Remus' is the first of several stories from Livy, Book 1. Livy (*c.* 65 BC–17 AD) wrote his history in 145 volumes, 35 of which survive. He says in his preface that he does not necessarily accept these stories as factually true, but he feels that it is appropriate that the gods should be concerned with the early days of a city that was to become the greatest in the world. By including these stories, we aim to give an impression of Roman traditions and values, as well as to begin a skeletal outline of Roman history up to the time of Horace.

Romulus and Remus were thought to be the children of Mars and they were also, through Aeneas, descended from Venus. It would be worth asking your pupils what their descent from these two gods tells us about the basic nature of the Romans.

Sources
p. 78, para. 2: a Vestal Virgin: six Vestal Virgins were chosen by the Pontifex Maximus to serve the goddess Vesta and tend the sacred fire (which Aeneas had carried from Troy to Rome: see note on ch. 11, 'Aeneas tells of the fall of Troy', line 11). They were selected from girls aged between six and ten and served for thirty years, after which they might marry. If they were proved unchaste during their period of service they were entombed alive.

Illustrations

p. 73: the details in this reconstruction of the death of Dido reflect Virgil's description (*Aeneid* 4.645–50): 'she climbed the high pyre in a frenzy and unsheathed the Trojan sword for which she had asked – though not for this purpose. Then her eyes lit on the Trojan clothes and the bed she knew so well, and... she lay down on the bed' (trans. David West).

p. 76: this statue of Mercury by Giambologna (1529–1608) is Renaissance in period but Classical in feeling. Blown aloft by a cherub-faced wind, he has wings on his hat and his ankles and he holds his caduceus, a staff with two serpents twining round it. (Louvre, Paris)

p. 77: part of the mosaic floor of the *frigidārium* from Low Ham in Somerset (fourth century AD) which tells the story of Dido and Aeneas. (Taunton Castle Museum, Somerset)

p. 78: this personification of the river Tiber shows the river god (with reeds in his hair and holding an oar) in a protective posture over Romulus and Remus who are being suckled by a wolf. (Louvre, Paris)

p. 79: the 'Capitoline Wolf' is an intensely moving Etruscan bronze from the late sixth or early fifth century BC. It used to stand on the Capitol. The twins were added in the fifteenth century. (Capitoline Museums, Rome)

Chapter 13

In the last chapters of Part I, three of the narratives are stories such as parents might have told their children, though admittedly the story of Cupid and Psyche is anachronistic, since its author, Apuleius, lived in the 2nd century AD. This story comes from the only Latin novel surviving complete. It is concerned with the adventures of one Lucius, who dabbled in black magic and, anointing himself with an ointment which he was told would give him wings, he suddenly found himself turned into an ass (hence the title *The Golden Ass*). In his metamorphosed form Lucius was captured by thieves and endured many sufferings, being forced to carry the heavy burden of their spoils. At one stage the robbers captured a beautiful girl whom they held to ransom. When they went off to carry on their business, they left the girl in the charge of the old woman who cooked for them and told her to comfort the girl. As consolation the old woman told the girl the story of Cupid and Psyche.

This is the longest of all the stories from which *The Golden Ass* is strung together, occupying fifty printed pages. Our narrative is based on the first part only and omits amongst other things the evil machinations of Psyche's jealous sisters. In the second half Psyche undergoes a series of ordeals imposed by Venus and is eventually reunited with Cupid. Your students will be surprised by the romantic tone of the story even in its truncated form, more like a fairy story than the austere literature we associate with the Romans.

Cartoon captions

Students will not make much of the cartoon captions unless you tell them something of the context (see above).
1 **Cupīdō**: this is the first occurrence of a 3rd declension noun with nominative ending **-ō**; students will need help here.

Fābula trīstis

7 **nātū minimā**: literally 'the smallest (= youngest) by birth'.
8 **Psȳchē**: acc. **Psȳchēn**. Your students may ask about these forms, which are Greek. (The Greek word means 'soul' and some critics read the whole story as an allegory of the pilgrimage of the human soul, but we tell only half the story.)

multō pulcherrima: 'by much the most beautiful'; **multō** is 'ablative of measure of difference'.
20 **amōre flagrat**: 'burns with love'; your students have now studied the complete declensions of nouns, in which the ablative is said to have the meanings 'by, with or from', and so this phrase (glossed) should not give difficulty. **amplexū tenet** (line 32), 'holds in his embrace', may require comment.
25 **nōs tibi famulae sumus**: 'we are servants to you' = 'we are your servants' (dative of person concerned).

Respondē Latīnē

1 Venus Psȳchae invidet quod omnēs eam laudant et quasi* deam colunt.
2 Psȳchē trīstis est quod nēmō eam amat, nēmō eam in mātrimōnium dūcit.
3 Cupīdō Psȳchen per aurās vehit ad domum dīvīnam.
4 ubi Psȳchē ēvigilat, vōcēs audit sed nēminem* videt.
5 vōcēs dīcunt: 'nōs famulae* tibi sumus.'
* Students will need help with these words.

Psȳchē marītum perdit

3 **nōn licet tibi**: literally 'it is not allowed to you' = 'you are not allowed', 'you may not'; you may have to comment on the impersonal use of the verb. Encourage your students to make an idiomatic translation.
7–8 **gaudet complexibus**: **gaudeō** ('I rejoice in, enjoy') often takes the ablative case. As **complexibus** is glossed 'in the embraces' you need not labour this. Similarly **complexibus ardentibus tenet** (line 10, 'holds in/with his burning embraces') introduces an unfamiliar use of the ablative, sufficiently explained by the gloss.
13 **lucerna illa**: 'that lamp'; the demonstrative points to the lamp as the culprit, e.g. 'that naughty lamp'.

Grammar and exercises

Subordinate clauses
Simple subordinate clauses have been used freely earlier in the course and have probably caused no difficulty. But since much Latin prose is composed in more or less complex sentences containing several subordinate clauses, it is important that students should become used to handling them with facility. They must recognize all subordinating conjunctions immediately and know where each clause begins and ends; it may help in complex sentences to bracket off the subordinate clauses. However, this chapter does no more than make explicit what students have already met in their reading.

The relative pronoun and exercise 13.3

In Part I the relative pronoun is used in the nominative case only. The three genders singular and plural must be carefully learnt; **quae** is both feminine singular, feminine plural and neuter plural. This appears confusing at first sight but seldom causes ambiguity in context.

The main difficulty students are likely to encounter is in the word order such as that of sentences 7 and 8 in exercise 13.3. In these the relative pronoun agrees with object of the main verb which is placed at the end of the sentence; students may have to bracket off the relative clause, which leaves, e.g. in 7, the simple sentence **Quīntus amīcōs vocat**, and attached to **amīcōs** the relative clause **quī prope lūdum lūdunt**.

In sentence 10 **is quī** = 'the man who', cf. **ea quae**, 'the woman who', **eī quī**, 'the men who', etc.; you should call attention to this idiom, which is common.

Background: The Olympian gods

This section largely consists of unvarnished information about the gods and there is little room for discussion until the final three paragraphs. It seems to us appropriate to include the gods' Greek names in addition to their Roman ones. (Pupils may remember that Ulixes is the Latin for the Greek Odysseus.)

Most of the items that identify the various gods are mentioned in the pupils' text. You might mention these further items:

Juno is often portrayed with a peacock. This bird's plumage represented the eyes of Argos, the many-eyed giant whom Juno set to watch over one of Jupiter's former girlfriends.

Ceres is frequently portrayed with torches, a reminder of her search for her daughter Proserpina in the Underworld.

Minerva holds a spear and wears a helmet and aegis (a goatskin covering the chest with the Gorgon's head at its centre).

Apollo is often portrayed with a lyre or a bow and arrow (as a hunter). He might wear a wreath of bay laurel: it was the bay leaf that was chewed by his prophetess in the trances he inspired in her at his cult-centre at Delphi.

Diana's weapon, like her brother's, is the bow.

Mars wears armour and helmet. He carries a shield, spear and sword.

Reference to a good dictionary of Classical mythology, such as P. Grimal: *Penguin Dictionary of Classical Mythology*, Penguin, would prove valuable in this section.

p. 86, para. 1: the concept of sacrifice could be discussed, as could modern and ancient attitudes to the slaughter of animals for food.

para. 2: pupils could discuss the subject of whether

leading religious figures should give advice to politicians.

para. 3: we imply that many Romans were not deeply committed to their religion. It is worth discussing how committed we are today to the religions in which we have grown up. And how many of your pupils have grown up in no religion at all? What do they feel about that?

Illustrations

p. 82: to convey an idealized setting for Psyche's new home, we have used the Canopus from Hadrian's Villa at Tivoli. Arches and sculpture surround a man-made lake. As frequently with Roman villas, parts of the Emperor's country estate were named after famous sites and monuments of the East. Canopus is a suburb of Alexandria.

p. 83: this Hellenistic sculpture of the first century BC shows Cupid embracing Psyche. While the story presupposes that they are more than children, the statue insists on the youthfulness of the boy god of love and his girlfriend. It is known as the 'Capitoline Kiss' after its present location. (Capitoline Museums, Rome)

p. 84 (top): this famous bronze, dating from about 450 BC and found in the sea off Cape Artemisium in 1928, shows either Zeus (Jupiter) poised to throw his thunderbolt or Poseidon (Neptune) about to hurl his trident. (National Museum of Archaeology, Athens)

p. 84 (bottom, left): this votive relief of Athena (Minerva) was carved at Athens between 470 and 450 BC; she is portrayed as mourning for Athenians who have died in war. (Acropolis Museum, Athens)

p. 84 (bottom, right): the statue of Apollo is from a bronze original, probably of the fourth century BC. The god steps forward to see the effect of the arrow he has just shot. The graceful elegance and the strength of his body and his keen gaze have won much admiration. The statue is called the Apollo Belvedere because it is placed in the Belvedere courtyard of the Vatican. (Vatican Museums, Rome)

p. 85 (top): in this Hellenistic statue Diana is seen hunting, one of the spheres that define her as a goddess. (Louvre Museum, Paris)

p. 85 (bottom): Venus' adulterous relationship with Mars is encouraged by their son Cupid in this wall painting of the first century AD from Pompeii. (National Museum of Archaeology, Naples)

p. 86: this famous statue by Praxiteles dates from the third quarter of the fourth century BC. The god Hermes (Mercury) in the original statue dangled a bunch of grapes before the baby god of wine, Dionysus (Bacchus). (Olympia Museum)

Chapter 14

This narrative falls into two parts; the first introduces students to the ancient native Roman religion, which was probably more important to the Roman countryman than the official state cults; the second gives them a first glimpse of the Roman army, with echoes of the wider stage of Roman history on which Horace himself will soon perform.

Cartoon captions

The meaning of the captions is clear from the cartoons; students are likely to understand them without paying much attention to the reflexive pronouns. You could make this understanding explicit by looking again at captions 2 and 3; in 2, **canem** is the object of **exercent**. What is the object of **exercent** in 3?

Parīlia

2 **larārium**: the lararium was the chapel where statuettes of the Lares and Penates were kept, often no more than a cupboard (see illustration).

vīnum in terram fundit: the pouring of wine onto the ground (a libation) was the commmonest offering made to the gods; animal sacrifice was limited to very special occasions.

4 **Quīntus et Horātia**: the verb **prōcēdunt** must be supplied here. The same idiom is used in English: 'Flaccus goes to the field, the children (go) to school.'

5 **Parīlia**: on this ancient agricultural festival in honour of Pales, see the background essay. It is described in detail in Ovid: *Fasti* 4.721ff.

22 **imperātor**: 'the general'; the title was applied only to generals who had been hailed **imperātor** by their troops after a victory; Crassus had in fact not earned this title. Later the word comes to mean 'emperor', since Augustus and his successors monopolized the title.

27 **Crassus**: the invasion of Parthia, the great kingdom to the east of the Roman empire, was undertaken by Crassus from motives of personal ambition (he wished to compete in military glory with Pompey and Caesar); as he left the gates of Rome to join his army, he was cursed by a tribune of the people. He did indeed lead his soldiers to death at the battle of Carrhae (57 BC), where he was killed himself. Quintus was watching a dramatic moment in Roman history.

Quīntus mīlitēs spectat

4 **castra pōnere**: when a Roman army was on the march, a full-scale camp was constructed every night, which included tents laid out on a fixed pattern surrounded by a *vāllum* (ditch and rampart).

12 **ubi fuistī?**: 'Where have you been?' The 2nd person singular perfect form may worry students; the perfect is learnt in Part II, chapter 17.

17 **ī ... cubitum**: 'go to bed'; **cubitum** is the supine of **cumbō**, 'I lie down', expressing purpose after a verb of motion. Do not attempt to explain this to your students.

Grammar and exercises

Pronouns 1: demonstrative pronouns
Demonstrative, relative and interrogative pronouns, and a small number of other adjectives (**ipse, īdem, alius, alter, uter?, sōlus, tōtus, ūllus, nūllus, ūnus**), have genitive **-īus** and dative **-ī** (all genders); otherwise they decline like **bonus, -a, -um** (except for the nominative and accusative neuter singular of the following: **id, illud, īdem**). See Reference grammar.

Although **is** and **ille** are pronouns they can be used adjectivally, e.g.

> **illum/eum colōnum vocāmus.**
> We are calling that farmer.

> **illum/eum vocāmus.**
> We are calling that man/him.

It is important that students should understand the difference in use of **is** and **ille**, as illustrated in exercise 14.1.

Pronouns 2: personal pronouns
The personal pronouns are familiar to your students in the nominative, accusative and dative. The genitive is not common and the ablative has not occurred except with **cum**, when it is attached to the pronoun, e.g. **mēcum, tēcum, nōbīscum, vōbīscum**. We have glossed all such occurrences so far, but students should learn this idiom now.

nostrī and **vestrī** have alternative forms **nostrum** and **vestrum**; the latter are used only in a partitive sense, e.g. **uterque nostrum**, 'each of us'. We omit this complication at present.

mē, tē, nōs, vōs are used both reflexively and non-reflexively, e.g. **māter tē lavat**, 'mother is washing you'; **tū tē lavās**, 'you are washing yourself'. **sē** is used only reflexively and so has no nominative.

Exercise 14.2
7 **sibi sucurrere**: students should note the use of the reflexive pronoun here; it is used because it refers to the subject of the sentence. So also in 8 (**sēcum**), where **sē** refers to 'the women'.

Background: Roman religion

There is much to discuss here:

Why should the ancient native religion have had more appeal in the country than the city (p. 91, paras

1–3)? Can comparison be made with the modern world in this respect?

The homely, down-to-earth nature of the Parilia (p. 92, para. 2) may prompt a valuable discussion of analogous ceremonies or events in the religions that dominate the world today. There is a chance to put across the point that every religion contains elements that seem strange to an outsider (cf. the misunderstanding about Christianity referred to in p. 93, para. 1).

To what extent is it possible to separate religion from superstition (p. 92, para. 3)? What superstitious beliefs are prevalent today? How seriously do your pupils take them?

How cynical are your pupils about some aspects of their religions (p. 92, paras 4–5)?

The ability of Roman religion to accept and absorb other religions is remarkable (p. 93, para. 1). This should be stressed – as should be the paradoxical fact that the pagan Roman Empire was to establish Christianity as its state religion.

P. Jones and K. Sidwell (eds): *The World of Rome*, Cambridge, has a valuable section on Roman religion.

Question 1: this frieze, from a monument of the early first century BC, shows a purification ceremony being performed with the sacrifice of a bull, a sheep and a pig. A priest stands with his young attendants at the altar. To the left of the altar stands a soldier while to his left boys bring a bowl and a cloth for the purification. To the right stand three more soldiers. The monument is known as the Altar of Domitius Ahenobarbus and it is in the Louvre Museum, Paris.

Sources

p. 92, para. 2: the festival of the Parilia is described by Tibullus (2.5.78ff.) and Ovid (*Fasti* 4.721–862).

para. 3: the quotation is from Livy 21.62.

para. 4: the story of Publius Claudius Pulcher is told in Polybius 1.49–52, though the historian does not include the anecdote about Claudius' impiety. This is in Cicero (*De divinatione* 1.16; 2.8 and 33).

Illustrations

p. 88: in this *larārium* in the house of the Vettii at Pompeii, the *paterfamiliās* is in the centre, making an offering to the Lares who stand on either side of him holding drinking horns. (Alternatively, the man in the toga may represent the *genius* of the family.) Beneath, the sacred serpent is about to consume an offering laid out for it. (Since serpents live in holes in the ground, they have from very early times been thought of as vehicles for the spirits of the dead.)

p. 90: this frieze of soldiers marching is from Trajan's Column in Rome, which was dedicated in 113 AD to commemorate the Emperor's conquest of the Dacians (the inhabitants of modern Romania). Carved with a continuous spiral relief illustrating the Dacian campaigns, it is an unrivalled source of information about Roman warfare. The rectangular cavity is one of a number of 'windows' which let in light to the staircase, which coils up the centre of the column and is still in excellent condition.

pp. 92–3: for the sacrificial procession, see the Background section above.

Chapter 15

The stories in the last two chapters are taken from early Roman history; they illustrate the old Roman virtues of disinterested patriotism and courage which in the decadent times of the late Republic were told to Roman children as examples of the good old days.

Cartoon captions

Caption 3: for **obviam eī veniunt** see note on line 30 below.

Cincinnātus

The story of Cincinnatus is told by Livy (3.26–9). In 458 BC the consul was besieged by a neighbouring tribe, the Aequi; Cincinnatus was summoned from his plough and appointed dictator; he defeated the Aequi and rescued the consul and his army. He laid down his office within sixteen days and returned to his farm. For Livy, Cincinnatus was an example of the old Roman virtues of disinterested patriotism and simplicity of life, in contrast with the luxury and selfish ambition which had brought about the destruction of the Republic.

3 **quam fābulam**: 'which story?' The interrogative pronoun **quis**? has an adjectival form (**quī**, **quae**, **quod**, 'which? what?').

7 **mīlitiae perītus**: 'skilled in warfare'; **perītus** is one of the few adjectives which take a genitive ('the genitive of sphere of reference' – skilled in what? Answer, 'in the sphere of warfare'). The phrase is glossed; don't bother your students with this piece of information.

16 **patrēs**: the members of the Senate were regularly called **patrēs**: they were the fathers of the state.

21 **dictātōrem**: in the early Republic a dictator was sometimes appointed in an emergency; he was nominated by the consuls and elected by the Senate. He had sole authority for the duration of the crisis only; he resigned when he had done his job and the consuls resumed authority.

28 **togātus**: unglossed – to be guessed from the context.

30 **obviam eī**: literally 'in the way to him', which after verbs of motion means 'to meet him'. The preposition

ob with verbs of motion is used in early Latin to mean 'towards'; this meaning survived in verbs compounded with **ob**, e.g. **occurrō**, 'run towards, meet'.

Cincinnātus Rōmam servat

3 **et...et**: 'both...and'; the first occurrence of this use of **et** is liable to cause trouble, although it is listed in the vocabulary.

    cōnsulis: 'of the (besieged) consul'.

6 **ipsī**: this agrees with the subject in the verb – 'you yourselves'; students will be inclined to take it with **hostēs**.

Grammar and exercises

The irregular verbs 'volō' and 'nōlō'
volō means 'I wish, I want, I am willing to' (cf. **cupiō**, 'I desire' – a stronger wish). Draw attention to the infinitive **velle**.

    nōlō means 'I don't wish, I am unwilling', and often has the stronger sense of 'I refuse'.

Demonstrative pronouns
hic, haec, hoc (= 'this here') has the complication of adding **-c** to the case endings, which results in some alteration to spellings, e.g. **hun-c** (for **hum-c**), **han-c** (for **ham-c**), etc. (The final **c** of **hic** is an abbreviated form of the enclitic particle **-ce** which strengthens the force of the word to which it is attached; early and colloquial Latin use the forms **hice, haece, hoce**, etc.)

Background: From monarchy to Republic

More episodes from Book 1 of Livy. The key passage here is p. 100, para. 3. To what extent do your pupils share or respect the values that Livy puts forward in these stories?

    You may wish to supplement the incidents described here with others from Livy, Book 1. A. de Sélincourt's translation for Penguin is a good one. More accessible to younger pupils is a book that excerpts many of the highlights, R. M. Ogilvie: *Stories from Livy*, Oxford.

Sources
p. 98, para. 1: the Etruscans were a powerful people long established to the north of the Tiber; in the sixth century BC they extended their power southwards as far as Campania and according to tradition ruled Rome. The last king of Rome, Tarquinius Superbus, was Etruscan; he was expelled in 509 BC (p. 99, para. 5) but the Etruscans attempted to regain control of Rome, led by Porsinna of Clusium (p. 100, para. 2). The Romans just succeeded in repelling his attack and the new republic survived. In this connection comes the famous story of Horatius holding the bridge over the Tiber.

Illustrations

p. 95: this relief from the first century AD shows a farmer stooping under his wares as he drives a laden ox to market, passing roadside shrines. This is certainly not Cincinnatus, but the relief suggests the dogged agricultural virtues which he embodies. (Staatliche Antikensammlungen und Glyptothek, Munich)
p. 98: this noble statue of a general is in fact of Augustus and comes from Prima Porta near Rome. He wears his *palūdāmentum* (general's cloak) in a somewhat unlikely fashion: presumably the sculptor's intention was that the magnificent breastplate should be fully visible. The Cupid on a dolphin supporting the leg is a reference to his mother Venus, the legendary ancestress of the Julian family and thus of Augustus. (Vatican Museums, Rome)
p. 99: this moving bust, popularly identified with the Brutus who drove out the tyrants, is from the late fourth century BC. (Capitoline Museums, Rome)

Chapter 16

We end this Part with an extended comprehension exercise; no new grammar is introduced.

    The story of Cloelia, which shows that the Romans were not entirely sexist, is told by Livy (2.13). You will need to say a word or two about Porsinna and the Etruscan domination of Rome to set the context (see paragraph 1 of the background section to chapter 15 above).

Cartoon captions

These captions may present difficulties.
2 **foedus rumpitis**: the meaning of this is certainly not clear from the cartoon; give some help.
4 **statuam eius in equō īnsidentis**: 'a statue of her sitting on a horse'; this may be obscure. You will have to give some help. Equestrian statues do not seem to have been common in Rome and such a statue in honour of a woman is perhaps unique.

Cloeliae virtūs

virtūs: this originally meant 'manly qualities' (**vir-tūs**), especially courage; its meaning then extended to include all human excellence, including moral excellence, and so 'virtue'. Your students will gradually learn that over time words acquire different connotations and shift in meaning.
1 **haec**: 'these things', accusative neuter plural; but English says 'this'; compare lines 23 and 25.
2–3 **erat...praebuērunt**: the imperfect and perfect tenses are introduced in the first chapter of Part II, so a

preview of these tenses may be helpful here.

9–10 multīs nāvibus: 'with many ships'; students have learnt that the ablative can mean 'by, with or from', but they have not practised these usages and so might find this phrase difficult.

16 haud procul rīpā: 'not far from the bank'; the negative **haud** is commonly used with adverbs.

29 Sacrā viā: the Sacred Way was the road leading through the Forum up to the Capitol. The top of the Sacred Way was the very heart of Rome.

32 honōre dignae: **dignus**, 'worthy of', is followed by an ablative.

Background: Hannibal

In p. 104, para. 2, your pupils could extract the moral from the Regulus story. How sympathetic do they find him?

The saga of Hannibal is a tremendous one and could be left to stand or fall on its own strengths. However, further detail can be supplied from Livy: *The War with Hannibal*, trans. A. de Sélincourt, Penguin, or R. M. Ogilvie: *Stories from Livy*, Penguin. Two good books on Hannibal are G. de Beer: *Hannibal*, Thames and Hudson, and E. Bradford: *Hannibal*, Macmillan.

The most devastating commentary on Hannibal's achievement is provided by Juvenal in *Satires* 10. 417–67. This would be well worth reading out in translation.

Sources

p. 104, para. 2: Regulus: Horace praised him in *Odes* 3.5.32ff.

    para. 5–p. 105, para. 1: the quotation is from Livy 21.35.

p. 106, para. 2: Maharbal's rejected advice: Livy 22.51. The modern view is that Hannibal was right to reject this advice. He did not have the siege artillery to tackle the strong walls of Rome.

    para. 4: the story of Hasdrubal's head: Livy 27.51.

p. 107, para. 2: *dēlenda est Carthāgō*: the elder Cato had been sent on an embassy to Carthage in 153 BC where he saw how quickly the city had recovered from her defeat in the second Punic War. After this he repeatedly urged the Senate to strike against Carthage before she once more became a menace to Rome. It is said that he ended every speech he made in the Senate with the words '*dēlenda est Carthāgō*'. Eventually his policy prevailed and in 149 BC Rome declared war on a flimsy pretext.

Illustrations

p. 103: on the right the Pons Fabricius (62 BC) leads to the Tiber island, on which a temple to Aesculapius was dedicated in 293 BC. The bridge to the left, the Pons Cestius, dates originally from 46 BC. It was rebuilt in 1892. In the foreground is the single remaining arch of the Pons Aemilius, the first stone bridge over the Tiber, which was completed in 142 BC.

p. 106: this relief of an elephant is from a sarcophagus dating from *c.* 130–150 AD. Bacchic revellers ride on top of the elephant. (Fitzwilliam Museum, Cambridge)

p. 107, map: here we show not only Hannibal's route, but also the sites of his great victories over the Romans (Trebia, Trasimene and Cannae) and that of the Battle of Metaurus where his brother Hasdrubal was defeated and lost his life.

Appendix: Ciceronis filius

The purpose of this appendix is partly to provide a longer passage of continuous reading, which students who are making good progress can read confidently, and partly to give an introduction to a different social context; the story in Part I is bounded by the narrow horizons of the family of a freedman, a small-time farmer in a remote country town; the young Cicero belongs to a wealthy and important family, always at the centre of events.

Students should not attempt to read the story until they have completed chapter 11 and are familiar with all the cases. They should then be able to read it rapidly and continuously; it contains very few linguistic difficulties apart from vocabulary.

No words which occur in Part I are glossed and students must look up words as necessary in the General Vocabulary; but words which have not occurred in Part I are either glossed or should be 'guessed' from the context and English derivatives.

A chronological table of the young Marcus Cicero's life will help to keep events in perspective:

BC

106	Cicero senior born at Arpinum
76	Cicero marries Terentia
75	Tullia born
65	Marcus born; Horace born
63	Cicero consul
58	Cicero driven into exile by Clodius
57	Cicero recalled from exile
51	Cicero appointed governor of Cilicia; Marcus accompanies him to Cilicia
50	Cicero returns to Rome (November) [Marcus sent to school of Orbilius]
49	Civil war breaks out; Cicero joins Pompey in Greece
48	Caesar defeats Pompey at Pharsalus
47	Cicero returns to Italy and is pardoned by Caesar
46	Cicero divorces Terentia; Marcus sent to study philosophy in Athens

45 Tullia dies
44 Assassination of Julius Caesar (15 March);
Marcus joins the army of Brutus
42 Marcus fights at Philippi. After the defeat and
death of Brutus he joins Sextus Pompeius
39 He returns to Rome and is pardoned by
Octavian
30 He is consul
29 He is proconsul of Asia

Our story ends with the fictitious meeting of Marcus
and Quintus at the school of Orbilius in 50 BC. It is
taken up again in Part II chapter 20. All the events in
this table are historical except for the meeting with
Quintus.

1 **Cicerō epistolās dictat**: the year is 65 BC, a very
busy year for Cicero, who was starting his election
campaign. In July he wrote to Atticus announcing the
birth of his son in the first line: 'fīliolō mē auctum scītō
salvā Terentiā' ('Know that I have been blessed with a
little son – Terentia is in good health.') But all the rest
is concerned with his election prospects.
　Tīrōnī: Cicero's freedman Tiro was his secretary
and respected friend.
2 **pulsat**: 'knocks on'; not glossed (to be guessed).
7 **Arpīnumque**: Arpinum is a small town in the
Sabine Hills about 180 km from Rome. It was the
ancestral home of Cicero's family, who were *domī
nōbilēs* (local nobility); none of his family had taken
part in public life in Rome before Cicero himself. Their
villa is described by Cicero (*de Legibus* 2.2–3) as
originally *antīquō mōre parva* (old fashioned and
small), but it had been rebuilt on a grander scale by
Cicero's father.
　Tullia: Tullia, or Tulliola (little Tullia), as he called
her, was adored by her father. He was completely
devastated by her early death in 45 BC.
15–16 **ē cūnīs tollit**: by tradition a father acknowledged a new-born child as his own when he lifted him
up into his arms (see illustration on p. 41). The naming
ceremony in fact took place six days after the birth; the
eldest child usually took the same names as his father,
so that Marcus' full names were Marcus Tullius Cicero
(fīlius).
19 **ē tablīnō**: the *tablīnum* was properly speaking the
room where the family records (*tabellae*) were kept,
but in most houses it was the grandest room, opening
off the *ātrium* (hall) and opposite the entrance door. We
have called it the 'reception room', since it was here
that visitors were usually received.
22 **occupātus**: 'occupied by' (not glossed).
26 **cōnsul fit**: 63 BC.
30 **gaudetque...redīre**: 'he rejoices to return';
gaudeō + infinitive is not uncommon; students may
need help. *gaudeō* is also found with the ablative, e.g.

studiīs gaudet = 'he rejoices in/enjoys his studies'.
31–2 **fīliōque Quīntō**: Quintus Cicero, born 103 BC,
was three years younger than Cicero. He married
Pomponia, the sister of Atticus, and his son, also
Quintus, was born in 67 BC, two years older than
Marcus.
35 **aedibus**: *aedēs* is plural when it means a house (in
the singular it means 'temple'). (Students have met
other plural nouns with a singular meaning: *nūndinae* =
'market day', *castra* = 'camp', *epulae* = 'feast' and
cūnae = 'cradle'.)
35–6 **monte Palātīnō**: the Palatine hill was the
smartest area of Rome.
37 **officiīs fungentēs**: the deponent verb *fungor* = 'I
perform' takes the ablative; as the phrase is glossed,
this peculiarity need not be explained.
　clientēs: these were not clients in the modern sense
but humbler men who attached themselves to a patron
(*patrōnus*); they owed their patron certain duties
amongst which was the *salūtātiō*: they would call on
their patron early in the morning and escort him to the
forum, if required.
40 **longās epistolās**: Cicero's correspondence was
vast; sixteen books of letters to Atticus alone were
published after his death, sixteen books of letters to his
friends and family, three books to his brother Quintus
and two to Brutus.
45 **paedagōgus Graecus**: it was the usual practice for
wealthy Romans to employ a Greek tutor to teach their
children the language. All educated Romans were
bilingual.
49 **ubi venit aestās**: in the summer the heat in Rome
was intolerable and fever was rampant. All who could
afford it retreated to the hills. Cicero owned six or more
estates scattered round Italy and his family would go to
one of these.
55 **inimīcī**: Cicero's chief enemy was Clodius. As
tribune of the people in 58 BC he proposed a law
outlawing anyone who had put citizens to death without
trial. Cicero as consul five years before had executed
without trial some of those who had taken part in
Catiline's revolutionary conspiracy. Cicero immediately
hurried into exile. His goods were confiscated and his
house on the Palatine was destroyed.
63 **ex exsiliō revocant**: in August 57 BC, despite
furious opposition from Clodius, the senate at last
passed a decree recalling Cicero; he landed at
Brundisium on 11 August, and a month later he was
voted compensation for the destruction of his house in
Rome and his country villas.
70 **senātōrēs Cicerōnem ad Ciliciam mittunt**: in
51 BC there was a shortage of men qualified to govern
provinces; the senate decreed that any ex-consul who
had not served as governor should now do so. Cicero
was appointed to govern Cilicia and went there very
reluctantly.

76–7 clārās urbēs Asiae: for visiting the famous
cities of Asia, such as Ephesus, compare Catullus 46.6.
On leaving his tiresome job in the province of Bithynia,
he says: *ad clārās Asiae volēmus urbēs* (let us fly to the
famous cities of Asia).

77–8 provincia in magnō perīculō est: Cilicia, on the
eastern border of the empire, was adjacent to the great
Parthian empire, which was always considered a
menace since the defeat of Crassus at Carrhae (57 BC;
see chapter 14). Rumours of a Parthian invasion at this
time proved false, but Cicero had to ward off incur-
sions by tribes on the eastern border of the province.
He defeated them in several engagements and was
acclaimed *imperātor* by his troops. He wrote to Atticus
describing his campaign and ironically comparing
himself to Alexander the Great: 'For a few days I
occupied the same camp as Alexander had against
Darius at Issus, a general considerably better than you
or me' (*ad Att.* 5.20.3).

82 ā Ciliciā discēdit: Cicero left Cilicia in July as
soon as his year as governor was up and eventually
arrived at Brundisium on 24 November 50 BC. On his
arrival in Rome he found that civil war was now
inevitable; on 10 January Caesar crossed the Rubicon
at the head of his army and the war had begun.

At this point in our story we make Cicero send
Marcus to Orbilius' school. Cicero himself joined
Pompey in Greece; he returned to Italy after Pompey's
defeat (Pharsalus, 48 BC) and death, where he was
pardoned by Caesar and lived in semi-retirement,
writing philosophical works. Only after the assassination of Julius Caesar did he re-emerge into politics to
lead the senate's opposition to Antony.

Translations

Chapter 1

Cartoon captions

1 Quintus is a Roman boy.
2 Quintus lives in Apulia; Apulia is in Italy.
3 Scintilla is a Roman woman; she is working in the house.
4 Horatia is a Roman girl; she is dining in the house.

Scintilla and Horatia at home

Scintilla is working in the house; she is tired. Horatia comes into the house; she is hungry. But dinner is not ready. Scintilla hurries and soon dinner is ready.

'Look!' she says; 'dinner is ready.' The girl is glad; she hurries to the table and dines greedily.

The next day Scintilla walks to the shops. Horatia works in the house. Soon Scintilla returns and comes into the house. Look! dinner is ready. Scintilla is glad.

Exercise 1.1

1 The woman is hurrying/the woman hurries.
2 The girl is dining/the girl dines.
3 Scintilla is entering/enters.
4 Horatia is not working/does not work.

Exercise 1.2

1 Scintilla is tired.
2 The girl is happy.
3 Dinner is not ready.
4 Scintilla is a woman.

Exercise 1.3

1 *intrat*. The girl enters (into) the house.
2 *labōrat*. The woman is working.
3 *est*. Dinner is not ready.
4 *festīnat*. Scintilla is hurrying.
5 *cēna*. Soon dinner is ready.
6 *laeta*. Horatia is glad.

Chapter 2

Cartoon captions

1 Scintilla is working in the house; she is preparing dinner.
2 Horatia enters the house; she greets Scintilla.
3 Horatia is helping Scintilla; she is carrying water into the house.
4 Argus enters the house and greets Horatia.

What do the following sentences mean?

1 Horatia calls Scintilla.
2 Scintilla greets the girl.
3 The girl helps Scintilla.
4 Scintilla praises her daughter.

Argus steals the dinner

Scintilla is working in the house; she is preparing dinner; she is tired. Horatia is idling in the street. Scintilla calls her daughter. The girl enters the house and helps Scintilla; she carries water into the house. Scintilla praises her daughter.

Dinner is ready. Scintilla calls her daughter and tells a story. Horatia listens to the story happily. Soon Argus enters the house. He looks at the dinner; suddenly he snatches it and swallows it down. Scintilla is angry; Argus flies into the street. Scintilla prepares another dinner.

Exercise 2.1

1 *Horātia*. Horatia is working in the house.
2 *Scintillam*. The girl calls Scintilla.
3 *Scintilla; casam*. Scintilla enters the house.
4 *Scintillam*. Her daughter greets Scintilla.
5 *cēnam*. The girl prepares dinner.
6 *fīliam*. Scintilla praises her daughter.
7 *cēnam*. Argus enters the house and devours the dinner.
8 *īrāta; parat*. Scintilla is angry; she again prepares dinner.

Exercise 2.2

1 *vocat.* Scintilla calls her daughter.
2 *intrat; Scintillam.* Horatia enters the house and greets Scintilla.
3 *iuvat.* Horatia helps Scintilla.
4 *nārrat.* Scintilla praises Horatia and tells a story.
5 *laeta.* Horatia is happy.

Exercise 2.3

1 Horātia aquam in casam portat.
2 fessa est sed festīnat.
3 casam intrat et Scintillam vocat.
4 Scintilla fīliam laudat.

Chapter 3

Cartoon captions

1 Flaccus is a Roman farmer; he works in the field.
2 Flaccus brings Argus into the field.
3 Argus does not help Flaccus but sleeps.
4 Quintus enters the field. The boy calls Argus but Argus does not hear; for he is sleeping.

Quintus helps his father

The next day Scintilla calls Quintus; she sends him to the field. Quintus is carrying food to Flaccus; for Flaccus is working in the field for a long time and is tired. The boy hurries to the field; he takes Argus with him. Soon Quintus enters the field; he sees Flaccus and calls him. Flaccus hears his son and walks to him; he sits on the ground and eats the food.

Quintus does not return home but stays in the field and helps Flaccus. He climbs an olive tree and shakes down the olives. Flaccus collects the olives. Suddenly Quintus slips and falls to the ground. Flaccus is anxious and runs to him, but Quintus is not hurt; he gets up and returns home.

Flaccus praises Quintus

Quintus returns home and greets Scintilla; he takes Argus into the garden and calls Horatia. Horatia hurries into the garden; she is glad because Quintus is there.

Flaccus returns from the field; he is tired; he sits in the house and rests. Soon he says, 'Quintus is a good boy. He stays in the field and helps me.' Scintilla is glad because Flaccus praises the boy. She prepares dinner quickly; when dinner is ready, she calls Horatia and Quintus into the house. Quintus is glad because dinner is ready; he hurries into the house.

1 He sits down and rests in the house
2 Scintilla is glad because Flaccus praises Quintus.
3 Quintus is glad because dinner is ready.
4 *Scintillam*: acc., object of *salūtat*;
   laeta: nom., complement with *est*;
   puerum: acc., object of *laudat*;
   casam: acc., governed by *in*.

Exercise 3.1

1 Quintus enters the field and calls Flaccus.
2 The boy helps the farmer.
3 The farmer praises his son.
4 Horatia enters the house and calls Scintilla.
5 The girl helps the woman.
6 Scintilla praises her daughter.

Exercise 3.3

f., m., f., n., f., m., n.

Exercise 3.4

1 fīlia fessa est.
2 fīlius laetus est.
3 cēna nōn parāta est.
4 puer īrātus est.
5 fābula nōn longa est.

Exercise 3.5

1 *fābulam; laeta.* Scintilla tells a story; her daughter is happy.
2 *laudat; laetus.* Flaccus praises his son; Quintus is happy.
3 *colōnum; puerum.* The boy calls the farmer; the farmer does not hear the boy.
4 *videt; īrāta.* The girl sees Scintilla; Scintilla is angry.
5 *labōrat; fessus.* Quintus is working for a long time; the boy is tired.

Chapter 4

Cartoon captions

1 The boy sees the girl; he calls her.
2 The boys see the girls; they call them.
3 The girl hears the boy and answers.
4 The girls hear the boys and answer.
5 Argus is good.
6 Argus and Fidus are bad.

Scintilla and Horatia at the fountain

Every day when Flaccus goes to the field, Scintilla and Horatia hurry to the spring. They carry big water pots. When they come to the spring, many women are already there. Some are drawing water, others are carrying full water pots. Scintilla greets them and for a long time makes conversation/talks with her friends. Horatia plays with the girls. At length Scintilla draws water and returns home. Horatia also draws water and hurries after Scintilla.

The urn is big; Horatia carries it with difficulty. Suddenly she slips; the urn falls to the ground; the water flows out onto the ground. Horatia sits on the ground; 'Alas, alas!' she says; 'the urn is broken.' She calls Scintilla; she (Scintilla) returns to her and says, 'O daughter, why are you sitting on the ground? Get up and bring another water pot from the house.' Horatia gets up; she returns to the house and carries another water pot to the spring. She draws water and hurries home.

When Horatia returns home, Quintus is already on his way to school. He is walking slowly and often stops. Horatia hurries and soon sees him. 'Wait, Quintus,' she says. Quintus waits; Horatia runs to him. They go on to school together.

Flaccus goes to the pub

When dinner is finished, Flaccus goes out into the road and walks to the pub. When he enters the pub, he sees many friends. They greet him. Flaccus sits and drinks wine.

His friends talk (make conversation) for a long time; they are miserable; they make many complaints. Seleucus says, 'Oh dear! (Alas, alas!) It hasn't rained for a long time; the fields are dry.' Chrysanthus says, 'Food is dear; the farmers are miserable; but no one helps them.' Philerus says, 'The magistrates don't care about the farmers.' Others make other complaints. But Flaccus doesn't listen to (hear) them; he is tired; sometimes he sleeps, sometimes he drinks his wine. At last he gets up and returns home.

1 They are miserable and complain a lot.
2 They complain that there is a drought, that food is expensive, that no one helps the farmers, that the magistrates don't care about the farmers.
3 Flaccus takes no notice; he doesn't listen to them.

Exercise 4.1

nārrant, mittunt, sedent, dormiunt, vident, intrant.

Exercise 4.2

fēminae laetae, colōnōs īrātōs, puerī fessī, puellās miserās, agrōs magnōs.

Exercise 4.3

1 *puellae puerōs vident.* The girls see the boys.
2 *puerī fēminās audiunt.* The boys hear the women.
3 *fēminae filiōs laudant.* The women praise their sons.
4 *puellae fessae sunt.* The girls are tired.
5 *puerī labōrant.* The boys are working.
6 *colōnī filiōs dūcunt.* The farmers lead their sons.
7 *illae fēminae eōs iuvant.* Those women are helping them.
8 *puellae urnās magnās portant.* The girls are carrying big urns.
9 *puerī puellās vident.* The boys see the girls.
10 *puellae puerōs vocant.* The girls call the boys.

Exercise 4.5

1 Quintus calls Flaccus; he (Flaccus) does not hear his son.
2 Scintilla praises her daughter; she (Horatia) is happy.
3 The women lead their daughters to the spring; they (the daughters) are carrying big urns.
4 The boys see the farmers; they (the farmers) are working in the field.

Chapter 5

Cartoon captions

1 Quintus asks his friend: 'Why are you working in the field?' The friend replies: 'I am helping the farmer.'
2 Quintus asks his friends: 'Why are you working in the field?' The friends reply: 'We are helping the farmers.'
3 Scintilla asks Quintus: 'Why are you lying on the ground, Quintus?' Quintus replies, 'I am lying on the ground because I am tired.'
4 Quintus asks the girls: 'Why are you sitting in the garden, girls?' The girls reply: 'We are sitting in the garden, because we are tired.'
5 Quintus asks Scintilla, 'What are you doing?' Scintilla replies, 'I am preparing dinner.'
6 Horatia asks the boys, 'What are you doing, boys?' The boys reply, 'We are hurrying to school.'

Market day

The next day Flaccus and Scintilla get up early; for it is market day. Flaccus carries a great sack of wool; Scintilla puts olives and figs into baskets. Horatia is sitting in the garden. Soon Scintilla calls Horatia; 'What are you doing Horatia?' she says. 'Are you ready? We are going to market.' Horatia replies: 'I am ready; I'm coming at once.' Flaccus carries the wool, Scintilla the olives, Horatia the figs; they hurry to the forum.

When they arrive at the forum, many men and women are already there; throughout the whole forum there are stalls. The farmers are shouting and praising their wares. Some are selling grapes, some wool, others figs. Flaccus leads Scintilla and his daughter to an empty place; they put up their stall and display (put out) their wares.

Soon a friend approaches the stall and greets Flaccus; he looks at the wool. Flaccus says, 'The wool is good and not dear. I am selling the whole sack for three denarii.' The friend says, 'You are asking too much, Flaccus; I give two denarii.' Flaccus agrees and hands over the sack.

Meanwhile a woman goes up to Scintilla and says, 'How much are the olives?' She answers: 'I'm selling those olives for one denarius.' The woman buys the olives. Another woman comes up and looks at the figs for a long time. Horatia asks: 'Why are you looking at the figs like that?' She says 'I am looking at those figs like that because they are bad.' Horatia is angry and answers, 'What are you saying? We don't sell bad figs. The figs are good.' But the woman does not buy the figs.

Soon they sell all their wares. Scintilla is delighted and says, 'We have sold all our wares; now I'm going to the fish stall.'

Playlet: To the fish stall

Characters: Scintilla, Flaccus, Horatia, Fisherman

Scintilla leads Flaccus and her daughter to the fish stall.

Flaccus: What are you doing, Scintilla? Where are you hurrying? Fish are dear.
Scintilla: I'm buying a good dinner. Fish are not very dear.

Flaccus goes up to the stall and looks at the fish for a long time.

Fisherman: What are you doing? Why are you looking at the fish like that?
Flaccus: The fish are bad, fisherman. They stink.
Fisherman: What are you saying? The fish don't stink. They are good.
Scintilla: Be quiet, Flaccus. The fish don't stink. Fisherman, how much are these fish?
Fisherman: I'm selling those fish for one denarius.
Horatia: You are asking too much, fisherman.
Scintilla: Be quiet, Horatia. He's not asking too much. I'm buying the fish.

She hands over one denarius and takes the fish.

Horatia: Are we going home now? I'm starving.
Scintilla: We are going home. Soon we shall dine well.
Flaccus: We shall dine well, but how expensive that dinner will be!

Exercise 5.1

1 We are helping Flaccus.
2 I am hurrying to school.
3 He/she sees Quintus.
4 You are staying in the road.
5 They are sleeping in the house.
6 I am running to the field.
7 We warn the boys.
8 Why are you sending the girl to the field?
9 We are happy.
10 You are miserable.

Exercise 5.3

1 *facitis*; *parāmus*. What are you doing, girls? We are preparing dinner.
2 *festīnās*; *veniō*. Why aren't you hurrying, Quintus? I am not coming late.
3 *sedētis*; *sedēmus*; *sumus*. Why are you sitting in the road, friends? We are sitting in the road because we are tired.
4 *est*; *vocō*; *redit*. Argus is naughty; I am calling him but he does not come back.
5 *nārrās*; *sum*. Why aren't you telling us a story? I am not telling a story because I am sad.

Exercise 5.4

1 *miserī*; *laetae*. Why are you miserable, boys? The girls are happy.
2 *īrāta*; *parātī*. Scintilla is angry; for the boys are not ready.
3 *fessī*. We are tired because we have been (are) working a long time.
4 *ānxia*. Why are you anxious, Scintilla?
5 *ānxia*; *misera*. I am anxious because Horatia is unhappy.

Exercise 5.5

1 puerō fessō. 2 magnā casā. 3 multīs fēminīs.
4 puellā laetā. 5 colōnīs miserīs.

Exercise 5.6

1 *in agrō*. Flaccus and his son are working in the field.

2 *in viā; in casam*. The girls are playing in the road; Scintilla calls them into the house.

3 *ad agrum*. Flaccus leads the boys to the field.

4 *cum fēminīs*. Many girls are walking to the spring with the women.

5 *cum amīcīs/cum amīcō; ad lūdum*. The boy is hurrying to school with his friend(s).

Exercise 5.7

1 colōnus puerōs in agrum vocat.

2 in agrō manent et labōrant.

3 puer fessus est et mox ab agrō redit.

4 fēminae ad casam ambulant.

5 puellae cum fēminīs ambulant.

Chapter 6

Cartoon captions

1 The girls and boys wait near the door; the master tells them to come in and sit down.

2 The boys want to play. The master says: 'You must work.'

3 Decimus writes his letters badly; the master tells him to write the letters again.

4 At last the children are working hard; the master decides to tell a story.

The school of Flavius

Quintus is walking slowly to school and often stops, but Horatia goes on quickly; she arrives first and greets the girls who are waiting near the door. She has a long talk with Julia, a very pretty girl. Quintus sees a friend on the way, called Gaius; he calls him. Gaius is hurrying to school, but when he hears Quintus, he stops and says, 'What are you doing, Quintus? You ought to hurry; you are coming late to school. I am hurrying.' Quintus replies: 'We are not coming late, Gaius.' He tells Gaius to wait. He (Gaius) is anxious but waits. And so Quintus and Gaius go on slowly to school.

The other children are already there. The master comes out of the door and tells them to come in and sit down. The boys want to play, the girls want to work. The master, when he sees neither Quintus nor Gaius, is angry and shouts: 'Why aren't Quintus and Gaius here? Why are they coming late?' At last in come Quintus and Gaius and greet the master. But he shouts: 'Why are you coming late? You are bad boys.' He tells them to sit down quickly.

For a long time the children sit and listen to the master; for a long time the master shouts and teaches letters. The children write the letters on their tablets; the master looks at the tablets and corrects the letters.

Decimus, a big and stupid boy, learns the letters with diffculty. The master tells him to bring his tablet to him; he looks at the tablet. 'Decimus,' he says, 'you are an ass; you don't write the letters correctly.' Decimus says, 'You are wrong, master; I am not an ass. I do write the letters correctly. Look!' He writes the letters again. But Flavius says, 'You are impudent, Decimus, and an ass. You do not write the letters correctly.'

For a long time the children work. At last Julia says, 'We are working hard, master; we are writing the letters well; we are tired. And so you should send us off home.'

Flavius looks at her kindly. 'Yes,' he says, 'you are working hard, children. And so I order you to go off home at once.' The rest hurry home happily, but Flavius tells Decimus to stay in the school. 'You, Decimus,' he says, 'must write the letters again.' And so Decimus sits miserably in the school while the rest are playing in the road.

Flavius decides to tell a story

The next day Quintus and Horatia and Gaius arrive at school early, but Decimus arrives late. Flavius says, 'Why are you coming to school late?' Decimus replies: 'You are wrong, master. I am not coming late. The others arrive too early.' Flavius is angry: 'You are impudent, Decimus,' he says. He tells him to sit down and work hard.

Soon the children are writing their letters; they work hard. At last Horatia says, 'Master, we are working hard and (have been) writing our letters for a long time. We are tired. And so you should tell us a story.' Flavius says, 'Yes, you are working hard. Because you are good children, I am willing to tell a story.' He tells them to attend and listen to him.

1 They work hard, writing their letters.

2 Horatia asks Flavius to tell them a story.

3 He agrees to tell a story since they are working well and are tired.

Exercise 6.1

1 We want to play in the road.

2 You ought to hurry to school.

3 The master tells the children to come in quickly.

4 The children do not want to work.

5 The master decides to send the children away.

Exercise 6.2

1 *iuvāre*. The boys want to help the girls.

2 *procēdere*. But the girls tell the boys to go on to school.

3 *facere*. What do you want to do, girls?

4 *manēre*; *lūdere*. We want to stay in the road and play.

5 *sedēre*; *audīre*. We must sit in the school and listen to the master.

Exercise 6.3

1 cūr fessa es, Horātia?
2 cūr nōn Flaccum iuvās, Quīnte?
3 ad lūdum festīnāmus, Flacce.
4 cūr lentē ambulātis, puerī?
5 ānxius sum, ō fīlī.
6 cūr īrātae estis, puellae?

Exercise 6.4

1 Why aren't you hurrying, Quintus?
2 Who is helping Scintilla?
3 What are you doing, son?
4 How big is the field?
5 Are you taking me home?
6 Aren't you taking me home?

Exercise 6.6 (A revision exercise)

1 The friends are going to school slowly. They arrive late.
2 When they enter the school, the master is angry.
3 'Why are you arriving late?' he says; 'you are bad boys.'
4 The children sit and listen to the master; he teaches letters.
5 At last he decides to dismiss the children; he tells them to run home.
6 The girls are going to the fountain with Scintilla.
7 Horatia is carrying a big water pot and walks slowly.
8 Scintilla tells Horatia to hurry. 'Why are you walking slowly?' she says; 'you must hurry.'
9 When they reach the fountain, they draw water.
10 Horatia is tired; 'Aren't we going home now?' she says.

Exercise 6.7

1 quid facis, Quīnte? cūr nōn colōnum iuvās?
2 dīligenter labōrō; fessus sum.
3 quid facis, Horātia? ad forum prōcēdimus. nōnne parāta es?
4 parāta sum. veniō celeriter.
5 Flaccus fīlium iubet ad agrum sēcum venīre.
6 'Quīnte,' inquit, 'in agrō labōrāre dēbēs.'
7 nōnne cupis mē iuvāre?
8 sed puer fessus est; labōrāre nōn cupit.
9 tandem Flaccus cōnstituit puerum domum mittere.
10 Quīntus domum festīnat et Horātiam vocat.

Chapter 7

Cartoon captions

1 Quintus leads his dog into the field and greets his father.
2 Father and son are returning home from the field with the dog.
3 On the way Quintus sees many comrades; they all greet him.
4 Father takes the dog home, but Quintus plays with his comrades.

Flavius' story: The siege of Troy

Agamemnon, king of Mycenae, calls together all the princes of the Greeks; he orders them to prepare war against the Trojans. His brother Menelaus is there; Achilles, the bravest of the heroes, comes from Thessaly; Odysseus is there from Ithaca with his comrades, and many others. They prepare a great army and many ships. They sail to the city (of) Troy and attack the Trojans.

But the Trojans defend their city bravely. For ten years the Greeks besiege the city but cannot take it. At last Agamemnon and Achilles fall into a quarrel. Achilles is angry; he no longer fights but stays near the ships, idle. Now the Trojans conquer the Greeks and drive them to their ships.

Agamemnon sends friends to Achilles who tell him to return to the fight. They say, 'Achilles, the Trojans are conquering us and driving us to the ships. We are in great danger. You must return to battle and defend your comrades.' But he does not listen to his friends nor does he cease from his anger.

Soon the Trojans are attacking the ships and setting fire to them. Patroclus, a dear friend, goes to Achilles and says, 'Now the Trojans are burning our ships; you must cease from your anger and help your friends. If you refuse to fight, you must send me into battle with your comrades.' And so Achilles unwillingly sends Patroclus into battle. He (Patroclus) puts on the arms of Achilles and leads his comrades into battle.

When the Trojans see the arms of Achilles, they are terrified and flee to the city. Patroclus runs at them and kills many. But Hector, the bravest of the Trojans, stands firm and calls Patroclus into battle. He hurls his spear and kills Patroclus.

Playlet: The school of Flavius

Characters: Flavius (master); Quintus, Decimus, Gaius (boys); Horatia, Julia (girls)

Flavius is waiting for the children in the school. The children come in and greet the master.

Children: Greetings, master.

Flavius: Greetings, children. Come in quickly and sit down.

All the children sit down and are silent.

Flavius: Today, children, you must work hard and write your letters well.

All the girls work, but Gaius does not work; he looks at Julia.

Gaius: (*whispers*) Julia, won't you come home with me today?

Julia: (*whispers*) Be quiet, Gaius. Flavius is looking at us.

Flavius: What are you doing, Gaius? Why aren't you working?

Gaius: Me, master? I am working hard and writing the letters well.

Flavius: Come here, Gaius. I want to see your tablet.

Gaius goes to Flavius.

Gaius: Look, master! I am writing the letters well.

Flavius: You are not writing the letters well, Gaius. You are lazy.

Gaius returns to his seat and works for a little. Horatia has already written all the letters and is drawing pictures on her tablet. Flavius goes up to her and looks at the tablet.

Flavius: Horatia, what are you doing?

Horatia: I am writing letters, master. Look.

Flavius: You aren't writing letters but pictures. You are lazy. Write the letters again.

Quintus, who has already written all the letters, is idling. Suddenly he sees Scintilla through the window. She is leading Argus through the street.

Quintus: (*whispers*) Argus, good dog, come here!

Argus hears Quintus; he runs to the window and barks. Flavius hurries to the window.

Flavius: Go away, bad dog. What are you doing? Go away at once.

Argus jumps through the window and greets Quintus. Then he runs through the school room and looks for Horatia. All the children get up and chase Argus. Flavius despairs.

Flavius: Go away, children. I dismiss you. You, Quintus, take that dog out of the school.

Exercise 7.1

1	magnam urbem	1	bonō rēge
2	rēgem fortem	2	puerō fortī
3	nāvem longam	3	omnibus comitibus
4	mātrēs laetās	4	prīncipe trīstī
5	omnēs puellās	5	urbibus multīs

Exercise 7.2

1 *patrem.* Quintus call his father.
2 *fīlium fortem.* The father praises his brave son.
3 *mātre.* Horatia returns home with her mother.
4 *fessam.* The mother helps her tired daughter.
5 *urbem.* The Trojans defend the city bravely.
6 *nāvēs.* The Greeks cannot defend their ships.
7 *omnibus comitibus.* Patroclus runs into battle with all his comrades.
8 *omnēs; urbem.* All the Trojans flee into the city.
9 *urbem; Patroclum.* Hector does not flee into the city but attacks Patroclus.
10 *hastam; Patroclum.* He throws his spear and kills Patroclus.

Exercise 7.3

1	I enter	11	I go
2	we enter	12	we return
3	to enter	13	to go away
4	you (*s.*) enter	14	they go in
5	they enter	15	you (*s.*) approach
6	you (*s.*) sit	16	we can
7	you (*pl.*) sit	17	he/she can
8	we sit	18	I can
9	to sit	19	to be able
10	I sit	20	they can

Exercise 7.4

1 nāvēs parātae sunt. Agamemnōn nāvigāre iam cupit.
2 cūr manēs (manētis)? ad nāvem celeriter (ad)īre dēbēmus.
3 nōn possum nāvem vidēre. cūr nōn adest?
4 ecce! nāvis iam ā terrā abit; in illā nāve nāvigāre nōn potes (potestis).
5 prīncipēs tē iubent domum redīre.
6 crās in aliā nāve nāvigāre possumus.

Chapter 8

Cartoon captions

1 The children are waiting near the door of the school; the master says: 'Come in, children, and sit down.'
2 Quintus arrives late; the master says: 'Why are you arriving late, Quintus? Come in quickly and sit down.'

3 The children are sitting but not working. The master says: 'Don't play, children, but listen.'
4 The master comes to Horatia and says: 'Horatia, don't draw pictures on your tablet.'

The death of Hector

When Patroclus is dead, Achilles mourns for him for a long time; he wants to take vengeance on Hector. He returns to battle and leads his comrades against the Trojans. When they see Achilles, they are terrified; they flee into the city. Hector alone stays outside the walls.

His father Priam, king of Troy, and his mother Hecuba see him from the walls; they call their son. Priam shouts: 'Hector, don't challenge (call) Achilles to battle; you cannot conquer him. Come into the city. Be quick.' His mother shouts: 'Dear son, don't stay outside the walls; don't go to meet your death; your poor mother begs you.'

But Hector does not listen to them; he refuses to enter the city. He calls the Trojans and says, 'Shut the gates, Trojans; hurry. I am staying alone outside the walls and challenging Achilles to battle.'

The Trojans unwillingly shut the gates. Hector waits for Achilles alone. He comes nearer. Then Hector is suddenly afraid. He turns his back and flees.

Achilles runs quickly but cannot catch him. Three times round the walls flees Hector, but at last he stands firm; he turns round and calls Achilles to battle. Achilles advances and hurls his spear at Hector. But Hector avoids the spear. Then Hector hurls his spear and strikes Achilles' shield. But Achilles is unharmed; his shield saves him.

Then Achilles hurls his spear with all his might. The spear flies through the air and pierces Hector. He falls to the ground dead.

Achilles runs up and does a terrible deed. He ties the dead Hector to his chariot and drags him round the walls. His father and mother watch from the walls. Hecuba shouts: 'O Achilles,' she says, 'at last cease from your anger. Give us back our son.' But Achilles does not listen to her; he drags Hector to the ships and leaves him lying on the ground.

The ransom of Hector

For a long time his mother mourns her dead son; for a long time Andromache, Hector's wife, mourns; for a long time Priam mourns. At last, when night comes, Priam goes out of the city and goes on alone to the ships of the Greeks. The god Mercury guides him through the watchmen of the Greeks. At length he reaches Achilles' tent; he goes in and greets Achilles; he bows to the ground and says, 'O Achilles, I beseech you; cease at last from your anger and send back to his unhappy mother our dead son.'

When Achilles sees Priam, he is astonished. He is moved by pity; he lifts Priam from the ground. He gives (him) back his dead son and sends the father back to the city of Troy unharmed.

1 He goes alone to the Greek camp.
2 The god Mercury guides him.
3 He bows to the ground and begs Achilles to cease from his anger and return his son's body.
4 He is moved by pity; he raises Priam from the ground and gives him Hector's body.
5 (e.g.) Up to this point Achilles has been relentlessly cruel and pitiless; he now appears in a better light, merciful and humane.

Exercise 8.1

1 Come to the field, boys; don't stay in the house.
2 Go back home, Horatia, and help Scintilla.
3 Hurry to school, Quintus; don't play in the road.
4 Listen to the master, children; don't shout.
5 Sit in the house, Horatia, and listen to the story.
6 Hurry, Horatia; we are going to the spring late.
7 Come here, girls, and draw water.
8 Prepare the ships, princes, and sail to the city of Troy.
9 Attack the city bravely and conquer the Trojans.
10 Don't sit near the ships, Achilles, but defend your comrades.

Exercise 8.2

1 intrāte celeriter, puerī, et sedēte.
2 venī hūc, Decime; tabulam tuam vidēre cupiō.
3 dīligenter labōrā, Iūlia; nōlī lūdere.
4 dīligenter labōrāmus, magister; itaque fābulam nōbīs nārrā.
5 fābulam audīte, puerī; nōlīte clāmāre.

Exercise 8.4

1 *lūdum; amīcīs.* Quintus approaches the school with his friends.
2 *iānuam.* The master is waiting for the children near the door of the school.
3 *lūdum.* When he sees the children, he calls them into the school.
4 *lūdō.* At last he dismisses the children; they happily hurry home from school.
5 *agrum.* Quintus and Horatia are hurrying to the field.
6 *agrō.* When they approach, Argus sees them and runs out of the field.
7 *patrem.* The children are carrying food to their father.
8 *terrā.* He sits on the ground and eats the food.

9   *agrō*; *Argō*. Quintus stays in the field; Horatia returns home with Argus.
10   *casā*. When Scintilla sees her daughter, she comes out of the house and greets her.

Exercise 8.5

1   Quintus and Gaius enter the school.
2   The other children are already there and are listening to the master.
3   He is angry and says, 'Why are you arriving late? Come in quickly and sit down.'
4   Horatia goes into the garden; Scintilla calls her back.
5   'Come back, daughter,' she says, 'and come with me to the field.'
6   Horatia leads Argus out of the garden and runs back to her mother.
7   Mother and daughter hurry to the field with Argus.
8   When they arrive, Scintilla calls Flaccus. 'Come here, Flaccus,' she says. 'We are bringing your dinner to you.'
9   Flaccus approaches and receives his dinner.
10   Flaccus sends Horatia back home; but Scintilla stays and helps Flaccus.

Exercise 8.6

1   in agrō manē, Scintilla, mēque iuvā, sed Horātiam domum remitte.
2   nōlī mē domum remittere; cupiō manēre et cum mātre labōrāre.
3   itaque omnēs manent labōrantque in agrō.
4   Quīntus, ubi ā lūdō redit, in agrum festīnat.
5   ad patrem accurrit et 'tē iuvāre cupiō,' inquit; 'quid facere dēbeō?'

Chapter 9

Cartoon captions

1   The boy snatches the girl's dinner.
2   The girl snatches the boy's satchel.
3   The mother looks the girls' pictures.
4   The mother looks at the boys' tablets.
5   The son goes into his father's field.
6   The boy is carrying the dogs' dinners.

The fall of Troy

For ten years the Greeks besiege Troy but cannot capture the city. At last Agamemnon, king of the Greeks, despairs. He orders all the princes to assemble and says, 'For ten years now we have been besieging Troy; we often conquer the Trojans in battle but we cannot take the city. I despair. What should we do? Should we return home? What do you advise?'

The other princes are silent but Odysseus says, 'I don't despair. I have a new plan. Listen to me.'

All the princes listen intently to Odysseus' plan; they accept his plan joyfully. They make a wooden horse, huge; they send many brave men into it. These climb into the horse and hide themselves in the belly of the horse. The rest board their ships and sail to a neighbouring island.

At first light the Trojans see the ships of the Greeks going away; they rejoice because the Greeks are not there, they rejoice because fighting is at last finished. They run from the gates of the city to the deserted shore; they look at the huge horse standing on the shore. Some say, 'We must lead the horse into the city.' Others say, 'Don't trust the horse. We fear the gifts of the Greeks. Perhaps some Greeks are hidden in it.' At last they decide to lead the horse into the city. All joyfully drag it through the gates and place it in the citadel. Then they hold a feast and drink much wine.

Night is come. The Trojans are sleeping. The Greeks who are in the island board their ships and quickly return to the city of Troy. Those who are hidden in the horse silently go out (of it) and hurry to the gates.

The watchmen of the Trojans are sleeping; they are drunk. The Greeks kill them; they quickly open the gates and receive their comrades. They all run into the streets of the city. Few of the Trojans resist. Soon the Greeks capture the whole city. At last they attack the palace of Priam; they kill Priam and his sons. Few escape. So at last the Greeks take Troy and destroy the city.

Aeneas escapes from Troy

Few of the Trojans escape; they leave the burning city and flee into the mountains. Amongst them is Aeneas, a Trojan prince; he snatches his father and his wife and his small son from the flames and leads them to the mountains. Soon others come together to the mountains. All despair, but Aeneas says, 'Troy is burnt, but we Trojans survive. Come with me. We must found a new Troy in another land.'

They listen to Aeneas joyfully. They leave the mountains and descend to the shore; they board ships and soon they are sailing away from the city of Troy to unknown lands. For long they wander on the waves and undergo many sufferings. At last they come to Italy and found a city.

1   He rescues his father, his wife, and his small son and leads them to the mountains.
2   He says that although Troy is burnt, they survive and must found a new Troy in another land.

3   They sail to unknown lands, eventually to Italy;
    they suffer many hardships.

Exercise 9.1

1   *mātris*. The girl listens happily to her mother's
    story.
2   *puerōrum*. The master looks at the boys' tablets
    (the tablets of the boys).
3   *patris*. Quintus runs quickly to his father's field
    (the field of his father).
4   *fēminārum*. The farmer cannot hear the shouts of
    the women (the women's shouts).
5   *prīncipum*. Many of the princes want to flee into
    the city.
6   *Trōiānōrum*. Few of the Trojans are fighting
    bravely.
7   *urbis*. Hector flees three times round the walls of
    the city.
8   *Hectoris*. All the Trojans mourn Hector's death
    (the death of Hector).

Exercise 9.2

1   *fortiter*. Fight bravely, friends, and take the city.
2   *hūc; diū*. Come here, Quintus; your father has
    been (is) waiting for you for a long time.
3   *dīligenter*. Work hard, boys; the master is
    watching us.
4   *male*. Decimus write his letters badly; he is an ass.
5   *lentē; cūr*. Why are you walking slowly, Quintus?
    Why don't you hurry?

Exercise 9.3

1	to take	6	go away! (*pl.*)
2	we take	7	they go away
3	take! (*s.*)	8	to go away
4	you take (*s.*)	9	you (*pl.*) go away
5	I take	10	go away! (*s.*)

11 conquer! (*pl.*)
12 I conquer
13 to conquer
14 you (*s.*) conquer
15 they conquer

Exercise 9.4

1   fēmina prope portās urbis manet.
2   fīlius patris equum ad agrum dūcit.
3   puerī magistrī īram timent.
4   prōrās nāvium nōn possumus vidēre.
5   fābulam fēminae audīre cupimus.
6   potesne vidēre puellae mātrem?

Chapter 10

Cartoon captions

1   The Trojans sail to the shore of Sicily.
2   Mount Etna is throwing smoke and rocks into the
    sky; the Trojans are in great danger.
3   While they are resting on the shore, they see
    Polyphemus; he is descending slowly down the
    mountain.
4   Polyphemus advances into the sea and hurls rocks
    at the ships.

Polyphemus

Aeneas and the Trojans board the ships; they sail from
the city of Troy to unknown lands. For a long time they
search for a land where they can found a new Troy; they
undergo many sufferings, many dangers; often Aeneas
despairs. At last they decide to sail to Italy.

But when they approach Sicily, they scarcely avoid a
great danger; for they see the rocks where Scylla lives, a
horrible monster, and they hear the tremendous sound
of the whirlpool where Charybdis spews up the waves.
Father Anchises shouts in a loud voice: 'Flee; rescue the
ships from danger; for in those rocks lives Scylla.'
Aeneas hears his father's words and avoids the rocks. So
they scarcely escape from the danger unharmed.

When they come to Sicily, they see Mount Etna;
they steer their ships towards the land and towards
nightfall they reach the shore of the island. They rest on
the shore beneath the mountain. Mount Etna thunders
throughout the night; it hurls flames and rocks into the
sky. The Trojans are terrified and anxiously wait for
day.

They are hurrying to board their ships when they see
a man who is running to the shore. He calls the Trojans;
he runs up to them and says 'Save me, I beseech you. I
am a Greek, a comrade of Odysseus. The rest have fled.
I alone remain. Flee, unhappy men, flee. The Cyclopes
live here, vast giants, which eat men. Don't hand me
over to the Cyclopes. Save me. Receive me into your
ship.'

Suddenly the Trojans see Polyphemus, a vast giant.
He is leading his sheep down the mountain. He is blind;
he descends slowly; on the way he often slips. Aeneas is
terrified. 'Run to the ships,' he says; 'hurry!' The
Trojans take the comrade of Odysseus and flee to the
ships.

Polyphemus is now reaching the shore and advanc-
ing into the sea. He cannot see the Trojans but he hears
them rowing. He raises a huge shout. The other
Cyclopes hear the shout and run down from the mountains to the shore. They hurl huge rocks at the ships; but
the Trojans are already rowing from the shore. The
Cyclopes cannot reach them.

Playlet: Aeneas escapes from Polyphemus

Characters: Aeneas, First sailor, Second sailor, Greek, Polyphemus

The Trojans are resting on the shore of Sicily at the foot of Mount Etna.

First sailor: I don't want to stay here long; look at the mountain. It's hurling rocks and flames into the sky.

Second sailor: Look out! A huge rock is falling from the mountain. We can't sleep here.

First sailor: Look! someone is running down from the mountain.

Second sailor: I see him, a filthy, wretched man.

First sailor: Who is he? Aeneas, look out! A filthy, wretched man is running down the mountain towards us.

Aeneas gets up and looks at the man. The man approaches.

Aeneas: Hey! Who are you? What are you doing? Why are you running here?

Greek: Save me, I beg you. I am a Greek, a comrade of Odysseus. The rest have fled. I alone remain. Flee, unhappy men, flee. Huge giants live here which eat men. Save me.

First sailor: Don't talk nonsense. There are no giants except in children's stories.

Second sailor: Immortal gods! Look! That giant is not from a story.

Aeneas: Flee, friends. Run to the ships. And you, Greek, come with us.

The Trojans board their ships and row from the shore. Polyphemus comes down to the sea and advances into the waves. Suddenly he stops and sniffs the air; he raises a huge shout.

Polyphemus: Fee, fi, fo, fum,
I smell the blood of Trojan men.
Come, Cyclopes, hurry! Run down from the mountain. Trojans are here; hurry, unless you want to lose tomorrow's dinner.

The Cyclopes assemble and run down to the shore. They hurl huge rocks at the ships but cannot reach the Trojans. Aeneas stands in the stern of his ship and mocks the Cyclopes.

Aeneas: O silly Cyclopes, you are arriving too late. We aren't afraid of you. Look for another dinner. You can't eat us. Goodbye, blockheads.

Exercise 10.1

	accusative	*genitive*
1	puerum fortem	puerī fortis
2	multa saxa	multōrum saxōrum
3	puellās trīstēs	puellārum trīstium
4	magnum perīculum	magnī perīculī
5	silvās ingentēs	silvārum ingentium
6	nāvem celerem	nāvis celeris
7	altum montem	altī montis
8	omnia verba	omnium verbōrum

	ablative
1	puerō fortī
2	multīs saxīs
3	puellīs trīstibus
4	magnō perīculō
5	silvīs ingentibus
6	nāve celerī
7	altō monte
8	omnibus verbīs

Exercise 10.2

1 Flee, comrades; giants are throwing huge rocks against us.

2 Don't stay on the shore but run to the sea and board the ships.

3 It is time to row fast; now we are escaping unharmed from the danger.

4 But look at the sky, comrades; we are falling into a new danger.

5 A great storm is coming; we are always undergoing new dangers.

Exercise 10.3

1	he/she sends	6	to do/make	11	they return
2	send! (*pl.*)	7	they do	12	he/she returns
3	to send	8	do! (*pl.*)	13	return! (*s.*)
4	I send	9	you do (*pl.*)	14	we return
5	they send	10	I do	15	to return

Exercise 10.4

1 tandem Trōiānī ad Siciliam adveniunt et in lītore quiēscunt.

2 sed in magnō perīculō sunt; mōns Aetna saxa ingentia in caelum prōicit/conicit.

3 subitō Aenēās Polyphēmum videt. 'comitēs,' inquit, 'ad mare currite nāvēsque (et nāvēs) cōnscendite.'

4 Trōiānī verba Aenēae audiunt curruntque (et currunt) ad nāvēs.

5 Polyphēmus eōs audit sed vidēre nōn potest.

6 Trōiānī incolumēs sunt; nam in apertō marī iam nāvigant.

Chapter 11

Cartoon captions

1 Mother gives a new tunic to Horatia.
2 Father gives Quintus a dog.
3 The master gives their tablets to the children.
4 The children show the tablets to their parents.
5 Quintus gives the girls flowers.
6 The girls give the flowers back to him.

The meeting of Dido and Aeneas

While the Trojans are sailing from Sicily to Italy, a great storm comes; Aeolus, king of the winds, sends out all the winds. The Trojans are in great danger and cannot hold their course. At length the winds drive them to an unknown land. The Trojans get out of their ships and rest on the shore.

The next day Aeneas decides to explore the land. He says to his comrades: 'You stay near the ships; it is my intention (it is the intention for me) to go forward into the land.' With one companion he climbs a hill and looks out. He sees many men, who are building a city near the shore. Aeneas watches them for a long time. 'O lucky men!' he says, 'you are now building your city; we are always wandering on the waves.' At last he descends the hill; he enters the city and approaches a great temple.

On the walls of the temple are many pictures; when Aeneas looks at the pictures, he is astonished; for the pictures depict the Trojan war. He calls his friend and says, 'Look, friend, in this picture you can see Priam and Achilles. Here is Agamemnon. Look, here Achilles is dragging the dead Hector round the walls of the city. Do not be afraid. The sufferings of the Trojans are known to all.'

While he is looking at the temple, behold, the queen, called Dido, approaches with many princes. Aeneas runs to her and says, 'O queen, help us. We are Trojans who are sailing to Italy. A storm has driven us to your land.'

Dido looks at Aeneas, filled with wonder; then 'The fame of the Trojans' she says 'is known to all. Do not fear. I gladly help you.' So she receives them kindly and leads them to her palace. Then she calls all the princes of Carthage and all the Trojans to a feast.

When dinner is finished, Dido says, 'Come, Aeneas, tells us of the fall of Troy and all the sufferings of the Trojans.' All sit silent and look at Aeneas. He answers: 'Queen, you bid me renew unspeakable grief. But if you want to learn, hear the last sufferings of Troy.'

Aeneas tells of the fall of Troy

For ten years the Greeks besiege Troy, but we Trojans defend the city bravely. The Greeks cannot take the city. In the end they board their ships and sail into the open sea. We see them going away and gladly run out of the ciy; we rejoice because the war is over; we hurry to the camp of the Greeks; the camp is deserted, but on the shore stands a huge horse. We decide to drag the horse into the city. Then we have a feast and drink much wine.

It is night. While I sleep, the dead Hector appears to me in my sleep. He says, 'Flee, Aeneas; the enemy hold the walls. Troy is collapsing, you cannot save your country. Flee, and found a new Troy in another land.' So he speaks and hands me the sacred emblems of Troy.

When I hear Hector, I shake off my sleep. I climb to the roof and see the city burning. I take my arms and run into the streets. I meet many comrades who are wandering in the streets. I say to them, 'Come with me and attack the Greeks.' But we cannot resist the Greeks for long. Soon the whole city is on fire.

Suddenly the picture of my father comes into my mind. I run back home. Father and son and wife are waiting for me terrified. I tell them to leave the city with me. I carry my father on my shoulders; I hold the hand of my little son; I tell my wife to hurry on behind. We run to the gates through the enemy, through the flames. At last, when we reach the mountains, we stop. I look back, but I cannot see my wife. I run back into the city. For a long time I search for my wife, but in vain. At length I run back to my father and son. With them there are now many Trojans, who have escaped from the city. The next day I lead them to the shore. We find ships; quickly we board the ships and sail for unknown lands.

1 He suddenly thinks of his abandoned father.
2 Aeneas carries his father on his shoulders and holds the hand of his little son. He tells his wife to hurry on behind.
3 When he reaches the hills, he finds that his wife has disappeared.
4 Many Trojans who have escaped from the city are gathered there.

Exercise 11.1

1	bonae puellae	5	mātribus laetīs
2	fīliō cārō	6	omnibus lītoribus
3	regī fortī	7	parvō puerō

Exercise 11.2

1 Give me dinner. Give dinner to me.
2 I show you my father's horse. I show my father's horse to you.
3 I tell you all. I tell all to you.
4 The prince gives arms to the king. The prince gives the king arms.
5 The king gives him back the arms. The king gives back the arms to him.
6 Tell us a happy story. Tell a happy story to us.

7   I'm telling you a sad story. I'm telling a sad story
    to you.
8   The father gives his son a dog. The father gives a
    dog to his son.
9   The son shows the dog to his friend. The son
    shows his friend the dog.
10 The friend says, 'The dog is thirsty; you ought to
    give it some water / you ought to give some water
    to it.'

Exercise 11.3

1   fēmina aquam equīs dat.
2   pater fīliō cibum dat.
3   puer cibum patrī reddit.
4   māter puellīs fābulam nārrat.
5   rēx prīncipibus nāvēs ostendit.
6   colōnus canem mihi trādit.

Exercise 11.4

1   The Trojans resist the Greeks bravely; the Greeks
    cannot take the city.
2   Odysseus shows the princes a new plan; he orders
    them to make a wooden horse.
3   Agamemnon says to the princes: 'Odysseus is
    showing us a good plan; it is my intention to carry
    out his plan.'
4   The Greeks make a horse, just as Odysseus orders
    them; so the Greeks at last capture Troy.
5   The children are working hard; the master gives
    them a reward.
6   Quintus runs home and tells his mother
    everything.
7   Horatia runs to her brother and gives him a kiss.
8   Scintilla says to them: 'Hurry up, children; I'm
    preparing supper for you.'

Exercise 11.5

1   Horātia matrī in viā occurrit.
2   illa fīliae 'venī ad fontem' inquit ' et mē iuvā/mihi
    succurre.'
3   ubi domum redeunt, Quīntō occurrunt.
4   Scintilla cēnam puerīs parat; deinde fābulam eīs
    nārrat.
5   Dīdō magnam cēnam dat Trōiānis prīncipibusque
    Carthāginis.
6   ubi confecta est cēna, Aenēae 'nārrā nōbīs' inquit
    'omnēs labōrēs Trōiānōrum.'

Chapter 12

Caption

Dido takes a sword and pierces her breast.

Ill-starred Dido

When Aeneas makes an end of speaking, all sit silent. At
last Dido sends away her guests. Soon all are asleep. But
Dido cannot sleep. Through the whole night she turns
over in her mind Aeneas and the sufferings of the
Trojans.

Aeneas and the Trojans after such great sufferings
are very tired. They decide to stay in Libya and rest.
Meanwhile Dido begins to fall in love with Aeneas; she
always watches Aeneas; she hears and sees Aeneas even
when he is not there. Nor does Aeneas spurn the love of
Dido. Through the whole winter he stays in Libya and
helps Dido, while she builds her new city.

But the king of the gods, Jupiter, from heaven
watches Aeneas tarrying in Libya. He is angry because
Aeneas, forgetful of his destiny, is staying there. He calls
Mercury, the messenger of the gods, and says, 'Go now,
Mercury; fly to Libya. Bid Aeneas sail to Italy at once.'

Mercury prepares to carry out his father's orders; he
puts on his winged sandals and flies down from heaven
to Libya. He finds Aeneas building the citadel. He
approaches him and says: 'Hear me, Aeneas. I am
Mercury, the messenger of the gods; Jupiter, king of men
and father of the gods, sends me to you; he bids me say
this to you: Do not stay in Libya any longer, forgetting
your destiny. Sail at once to Italy and found a new Troy
there.'

When Aeneas sees Mercury before his eyes and hears
the warning of Jupiter, he is terrified. He cannot neglect
the orders of the gods. He returns to his comrades and
tells them to prepare the ships.

But Dido has learnt all; she summons Aeneas and
'Traitor,' she says, 'are you preparing to leave my land
without a word (silent)? Do you so spurn my love? Do
you leave me like this to die?' He, deeply moved, says,
'I do not spurn your love, nor am I preparing to go away
without a word. But Jupiter himself orders me to make
for Italy and found there a new Troy. I am not making for
Italy of my own will.' Then indeed Dido's anger flares
up: 'I don't keep you back. Go now. Make for Italy. But
I warn you: a terrible punishment awaits you. Sooner or
later either I or my descendants will exact vengeance
from you.' So she speaks and falls to the ground, in a
faint (senseless).

The death of Dido

Aeneas leaves Dido sad and moved and returns to his
comrades. He has to carry out the orders of the gods.

The ships are ready. The next day at dawn the Trojans cast off the ships.

When day comes, Dido looks towards the sea. She sees the Trojans' ships sailing towards Italy. She despairs. She orders her slaves to build a great pyre. She climbs the pyre. She takes a sword and, while all watch her terrified, she pierces her heart. When they see Dido dead, they are deeply moved. They mourn their queen and sadly light the pyre. The smoke rises to heaven.

Meanwhile, Aeneas, while he hastens through the sea, looks back at Libya. He sees the smoke rising to heaven. 'What do I see?' he says; 'Why is smoke rising to heaven like that?' But he cannot return. Sad and anxious he makes for Italy.

1   She sees the Trojan ships sailing towards Italy.
2   She despairs.
3   She orders her slaves to build a great pyre; she climbs the pyre and kills herself.
4   He sees smoke rising to heaven.
5   He has a foreboding that the smoke portends the death of Dido.
6   [The answer will be a personal reaction, not given in the Latin.]

Playlet: Aeneas deserts Dido

Characters: Aeneas, 1st Workman, 2nd Workman, 3rd Workman, Mercury, 1st Trojan, 2nd Trojan, Dido

Aeneas is lingering on the shore of Libya; he is building the citadel of Carthage for Dido.

Aeneas: Hurry, workmen. Carry the rocks to the middle of the city and build the citadel.
1st Workman: We are always carrying rocks. We are tired.
Aeneas: Don't idle, workmen. We must finish the citadel for the queen.
2nd Workman: We can't work any longer. It is midday. I want to lie under a tree and sleep.
Aeneas: Where are you going? I order you to carry those rocks.
3rd Workman: You don't rule us, but Dido. Dido always tells us to sleep at midday.
Aeneas: Go away, workmen, for a little; but come back quickly and finish the citadel for me.

The workmen go away. Aeneas sits alone on the shore. Suddenly Mercury appears to Aeneas and give him the message of Jupiter.

Mercury: Aeneas, what are you doing? Why are you lingering on the shore of Libya, forgetful of your destiny, and building the city for Dido?
Aeneas: Who is speaking to me? A god or man?
Mercury: I am Mercury, the messenger of the gods. Jupiter, father of the gods and king of men, sends me to you.

Aeneas: Why does Jupiter send you? What does he order me to do?
Mercury: Jupiter is angry with you, because you linger in Libya. He bids you hasten to Italy and found a new city for the Trojans.

Mercury vanishes. Aeneas is terrified.

Aeneas: What must I do? I cannot neglect the orders of the gods. I must hurry to my comrades and order them to prepare the ships.

Aeneas hurries to his comrades. They are resting on the shore.

Aeneas: Listen, comrades. Prepare the ships. We must sail at once from Libya.
1st Trojan: What are you saying to us, Aeneas? We are tired. We want to stay in Libya. Don't tell us to toil on the sea again.
Aeneas: Be quiet, friend. Jupiter himself bids us sail to Italy and found a new Troy.
2nd Trojan: What do you tell us? Jupiter himself bids us found a new Troy in Italy? Rejoice, friends. We are not afraid of winds or storms. Hurry to the shore and get the ships ready.

The Trojans go off happily. Aeneas remains on the shore, alone and sad.

Aeneas: What should I do? Dido loves me. How can I tell her the orders of the gods? How can I desert her?

But Dido has already learnt all; miserable and angry, she waits for Aeneas; when he arrives, madness and anger overcome her mind.

Dido: Traitor, are you trying to go away without a word? Do neither my love hold you back nor your word? Are you deserting me? Are you leaving me alone to die?
Aeneas: Don't blame me, Dido. I am leaving you unwillingly. I seek Italy unwillingly.
Dido: Traitor, do you thus despise my tears? Is it thus you repay all my kindnesses? Go now! I don't keep you back. Seek your Italy. Found a new city for the Trojans. But I warn you of this: since you betray me and spurn my love, expect a terrible vengeance. Sooner or later either I or my descendants will make you pay for this (will exact punishment from you).

Dido falls to the ground in a faint. Aeneas, sad and anxious, returns to his comrades and gets the ships ready.

Exercise 12.1

1   There are many temples in the city.
2   There is a huge rock on that shore.

3   Be diligent, children, and write your letters well.
4   There are many dogs in that wood.
5   Be quiet, Quintus; the master is looking at you.

Exercise 12.2

1   *ad Siciliam*; *ē nāvibus*; *in lītore*. When the Trojans reach Sicily, they go out of their ships and rest on the shore.
2   *dē monte altō*. The next day they see Polyphemus; he is descending from a high mountain.
3   *ad nāvēs*. The Trojans cannot resist him. Aeneas orders his comrades to flee to the ships.
4   *ad lītus*; *ā terrā*. When they reach the shore, they board their ships and row away from land.
5   *ad mare*; *per undās*. Polyphemus arrives at the sea and walks through the waves.
6   *dē montibus*. Suddenly he hears the Trojans and shouts to the Cyclopes: 'Come down from the mountains; help me.'
7   *ē lītore*; *in nāvēs*. They quickly gather and hurl huge rocks from the shore at the ships.
8   *ē perīculō*. But the Trojans row bravely and so escape unharmed from the danger.

Exercise 12.4

1   Aenēās, ubi Dīdōnem videt, ad eam accurrit et 'rēgīna,' inquit, 'succurre nōbīs.'
2   Dīdō eum benignē accipit; nam fāma Trōiānōrum omnibus nōta est.
3   dūcit eum ad rēgiam et magnam cēnam omnibus Trōiānīs dat.
4   post cēnam 'Aenēās,' inquit, 'narrā nōbīs omnēs labōrēs Trōiānōrum.'
5   omnēs tacitī eum audiunt, dum ille fābulam eīs narrat.

Chapter 13

Cartoon captions

1   While Psyche is sleeping alone under a tree, Cupid approaches.
2   While the girl is sleeping, Cupid lifts her and carries her through the air.
3   When Psyche awakes, she is astonished, because she hears voices but sees no one.
4   Psyche, who longs to see the face of her husband, prepares a lamp.

A sad story

Horatia and Scintilla are resting under a tree. Horatia says to her mother: 'While we are resting, Mother, tell me a story.' Scintilla replies to her daughter: 'What kind of story do you want to hear, dear daughter?' Horatia says, 'Tell me a sweet story, Mother.' Scintilla says, 'Listen daughter, I will tell you a story sweet but sad.'

Many years ago in a far off land live a king and queen who have three daughters; all the daughters are beautiful, but the youngest, called Psyche, is far the most beautiful. All men and all women praise her and worship her like a goddess. At length the goddess Venus is angry; she is jealous of the girl because she is beautiful, she is jealous because all worship her like a goddess. She summons Cupid and says, 'Dear son, you can rouse love in human hearts. Go now, search for a beautiful girl called Psyche. Shoot an arrow and force her to love some miserable and ugly man.'

Cupid prepares to carry out his mother's orders. He takes his bow and arrows and flies to earth. Soon he finds Psyche, who is sitting alone under a tree; she is sad; for all praise her, all worship her, but no one loves her, no one leads her into marriage. For a long time Cupid looks at that marvellous beauty. Psyche is now sleeping. Cupid draws near and looks at her closer. At once he burns with love. While the girl is sleeping, he lifts her up and carries her through the air to a divine house; there he gently puts her down on a bed.

Soon Psyche awakes and gets up. She looks at everything. She hears voices but sees no one. The voices say: 'All that you see, mistress, your husband gives to you. We are your servants. Enter, and dine.' Psyche is extremely astonished but enters the dining-room and sees dinner ready.

She dines happily. Then she sleeps. While she is sleeping, she hears a sound; she awakes; she is terrified. Her unknown husband is there. He ascends the bed and holds Psyche in his embrace; but before sunrise he goes away. When Psyche wakes up, she is alone; she sees no sign of her husband. The voices alone are there, which look after her.

Psyche loses her husband

The next night while Psyche is sleeping, again that husband is there and says, 'Psyche, dear wife, I love you deeply and give you all that you desire. But you may not see my face. If you see me in the light, I shall never return to you.' When Psyche hears her husband's words, she is very sad, but the kisses of her husband bring her consolation. Soon she sleeps, and when she awakes, she is alone.

For a long time Psyche lives like this: in the day time the voices care for her, at night she enjoys the embraces of her husband. But she longs to see her husband's face. And so one night she prepares a lamp. Her husband returns and mounts the bed; he holds Psyche in his burning embraces, then sleeps. Psyche leaps from the bed and lights the lamp; then for the first time she sees her husband's face. At once she burns with love; again and again she kisses the sleeping Cupid. But that lamp lets fall a drop of burning oil, which falls onto Cupid. At once Cupid leaps up, and never afterwards returns to Psyche.

1 In the day time the voices look after her, at night she enjoys the embraces of her husband.
2 She longs to see her husband's face.
3 She at once burns with love and kisses Cupid again and again.
4 A drop of burning oil falls onto him from the lamp.
5 He leaps up and never returns to Psyche.

Exercise 13.2

1 *While* Horatia is resting, Scintilla tells a story.
2 Horatia rejoices, *because* the story pleases her.
3 *If* you want to hear a story, be quiet and listen to me.
4 *When* Quintus returns from school, he also listens to the story.
5 The goddess Venus is jealous of the girl, *because* all worship her like a goddess.
6 *While* Psyche is asleep, Cupid lifts her through the air.
7 *When* Psyche wakes up, she sees no one.
8 Psyche is sad, *because* she never sees the face of her husband.

Exercise 13.3

1 Quintus, who is hurrying to school, meets a friend on the way.
2 Horatia, who is waiting for Quintus, is sitting in the road.
3 The women who are at the fountain greet Horatia's mother.
4 Odysseus explains to the princes his plan, which pleases them.
5 Aeneas hears the orders of Jupiter, which terrify him.
6 The Trojans, who now see Polyphemus, are terrified.
7 Quintus calls his friends, who are playing near the school.
8 Horatia meets the girls who are going to the spring.
9 The princes do all that the king orders.
10 The man who is helping us is not known to me.

Exercise 13.4

1 *quae*. Do you see those women who are hurrying to the spring?
2 *quī*. Bravely resist the Greeks who are attacking the city.

3 *quod*. Look at the sky, which is now clear.
4 *quae*. Don't fear the dangers, which are not great.
5 *quae*. Greet Horatia, who is waiting for you in the garden.

Exercise 13.5

1 dum lūdit Quīntus, Horātia labōrat.
2 sī lūdis, venī hūc et mihi succurre.
3 nōlō tibi succurrere, quod fessus sum.
4 Psȳchē, quae sōla sedet, trīstis est.
5 dum dormit, sonum audit.
6 ubi ēvigilat, nēminem videt.
7 Trōiānī ad lītus quod proximum est nāvigant.
8 Aenēās, quī terram explōrāre vult, comitēs in lītore relinquit.
9 collem ascendit multōsque videt quī urbem aedificant.
10 ad templa accēdit quae in urbe stant.

Chapter 14

Cartoon captions

1 Horatia is washing herself in the house. Scintilla says, 'Hurry, Horatia; get ready (prepare yourself) for dinner.'
2 Quintus and a friend are exercising the dog in the field.
3 The boys are exercising (themselves) in the garden. Scintilla says, 'What are you doing, boys?' They reply: 'We are exercising (ourselves).'
4 Scintilla says, 'Hurry up, boys. Get ready for dinner.'

The Parilia

Every day at first light Flaccus calls together the whole family and leads them to the lararium. He pours wine on the ground and prays to the Lares: 'O Lares, I beseech you, look after the family today and keep the flocks safe.' Then he proceeds to the field, Quintus and Horatia to school. But today Flaccus says, 'It is a feast day; get ready; we are celebrating the Parilia.'

All wash (themselves). Then Flaccus tells his family to come with him to the sacred place in which they have to celebrate the Parilia. Many people are hurrying joyfully to the fields, men, women and children. Horatia and Quintus greet their friends. There are many flowers near the road; the boys pick flowers and make garlands; they give them to the girls. At last they reach the sacred place. All remain silent, while the priest pours wine on the ground and prays to Pales: 'Kindly Pales,' he says, 'we beseech you; keep safe the flocks, look after the lambs; keep off diseases.' All sing a sacred song. Then they prepare a feast and dine joyfully.

After the feast they prepare (themselves) for the games. The young men make great heaps of straw. They set fire to the heaps. Flames ascend into the sky. The young men bravely jump over the flames, while the rest shout and applaud.

While Quintus is watching the games, up runs Gaius and says 'Come with me, Quintus. Soldiers are marching into the town.' Quintus, forgetful of his parents, runs with Gaius to the forum. When they get there, soldiers are already marching through the forum. First comes the general; he wears a purple cloak and riding on a white horse he leads the army; after him ride the officers. After them march the centurions and common soldiers.

Now many of the farmers are returning from the fields and watch the soldiers. An old man, who is standing near Quintus, says, 'Look! Crassus is marching to war, a rotten man. He doesn't care for the Roman people; he wants nothing except to increase his own glory. Without doubt he is leading his soldiers to death.' He spits onto the ground and goes off home. Soon the last of the soldiers are passing by and the farmers return home. But Quintus wants to see more. 'Come,' he says to Gaius, and hurries after the soldiers.

Quintus watches the soldiers

Crassus leads his soldiers out of the gates into the country. At length he turns round and raises his hand. The army halts. Crassus gives orders to the legionary commanders; they ride to the legions and give orders to the centurions. The centurions order the soldiers to pitch camp. They hurry to their tasks. Before sunset all is ready.

Quintus and Gaius are watching the soldiers from a nearby hill, forgetful of their parents. But Gaius says, 'Come with me, Quintus. Night is here. We must run back home. Without doubt our parents are anxious and angry.' The night is dark. They can scarcely see the way, but at last they reach the gates of the town.

When Quintus gets home, Scintilla and Horatia are sitting in the house, sad and anxious. Scintilla gets up and says, 'O Quintus, where have you been? Your father is looking for you in the fields. He is extremely angry.' Quintus tells his mother all and anxiously waits for his father. At last Flaccus returns. Scintilla runs to him and says, 'Flaccus, Quintus is here. He's safe.' Flaccus turns to Quintus and says, 'Where have you been, Quintus? You are a bad boy. Why do you worry your parents like this? Go now to bed.'

1   Because night had come and their parents would be anxious.
2   She was sitting in the house with Horatia, anxious and sad.

3   Flaccus was searching for Quintus in the fields.
4   'You are a bad boy. Why do you worry your parents like this? Go to bed.'

Exercise 14.1

1   *illa*; *eam*. Scintilla tells Horatia a story; she (Horatia) listens to her (Scintilla) happily.
2   *illī*; *eī*. The master tells the children to enter the school; they obey him.
3   *illī*; *eum*. Quintus meets his friends in the road; they tell him to stay.
4   *ille*; *eum*. Flaccus calls Argus; he (Argus) does not hear him (Flaccus); for he is asleep.
5   *illae*; *eam*. Horatia is waiting for the girls in the forum; they hurry to her.

Exercise 14.2

1   Scintilla prepares dinner.
2   Horatia prepares herself/gets ready for dinner.
3   The sailors turn the ship towards the shore.
4   The sailors turn (themselves) and greet us.
5   The boys are exercising the dog in the road.
6   Why are you exercising (yourselves) in the field?
7   The father tells his son to help him.
8   The women tell their daughters to come with them to the spring.

Exercise 14.3

ego mē vertō
tu tē vertis
ille sē vertit
nōs nōs vertimus
vōs vōs vertitis
illī sē vertunt

Exercise 14.4

1   Argus is a bad dog; he rolls in the mud and is extremely dirty.
2   Scintilla says, 'Argus is extremely dirty; you must wash him.'
3   Quintus says, 'O dirty dog, why can't you wash yourself? I don't want to wash you.'
4   Scintilla says, 'Get ready, children. You must wash your dog at once.'
5   Quintus turns to his mother and says, 'I'm busy; Horatia must wash her own dog herself.'
6   Horatia says, 'Don't be lazy, Quintus. Argus is not my dog, but yours.'
7   At last Quintus brings a pot of water and helps Horatia. For a long time they wash Argus.
8   As soon as (when first) they let him go, off he goes and rolls in the mud again.

Exercise 14.5

1 *sē*; *tē*. Scintilla turns to Horatia and says, 'Get ready for dinner, Horatia.'

2 *sē*; *mē*. Horatia, who is washing (herself), says, 'I'm coming at once; I'm getting ready now.'

3 *sē*. Quintus is exercising (himself) in the field; he is climbing a high tree.

4 *sibi*. Suddenly he falls to the ground; he tells his father to help him.

5 *vōs*. The soldiers are sitting in the field; the centurion says, 'Why are you sitting idle in the field, soldiers? Why aren't you exercising?'

6 *sē*. They get up reluctantly and exercise (themselves).

Chapter 15

Cartoon captions

1 While Cincinnatus is cultivating (ploughing) his field, messengers approach and order him to come to the senate.

2 He tells his wife to bring out his toga and hurries to the senate.

3 When he approaches the city, the senators themselves come to meet him.

4 Cincinnatus takes off his toga and again cultivates his field.

Cincinnatus

When Quintus and Horatia return from school and Flaccus from the field, they all rest. Soon Quintus says, 'Father, please (if you will) tell us a story.' He answers, 'What story do you want to hear, Quintus?' Quintus says, 'Tell me the story about Cincinnatus, father.' He replied, 'You've already heard that story often, Quintus, but if you want to hear it again, I am willing to tell it.'

Cincinnatus is a brave man and experienced in war, but poor; he cultivates a small field himself across the Tiber. At that time Rome is a small city; it is always waging war with many enemies. Once the enemy lead their forces into Roman territory and pitch camp not far from the walls of the city. The Roman consul, an inexperienced and timid man, leads out his legions and tries to drive back the enemy. He pitches camp on a hill near the enemy but is afraid to attack them. They quickly surround the Roman camp and besiege the army.

When the citizens learn this, they are very afraid. They gather at the senate house and tell the fathers (i.e. the senators) to save the city; they shout: 'The city is in great danger. Save our city, fathers. Drive back the

enemy.' The consul says to the fathers, 'What should we do, fathers? How can we save the city?' The fathers answer, 'Cincinnatus alone can save us, for he is experienced in war and is a brave man, who loves his country and always defeats the enemy. We must appoint him dictator. Summon Cincinnatus to the city at once.'

And so the fathers send messengers to Cincinnatus. They hurry across the Tiber and soon find Cincinnatus who is working in his field. The messengers approach him and say, 'Cincinnatus, the fathers bid you come to the senate at once.' He is very surprised but he cannot neglect the orders of the senate; he hurries home; he washes himself and tells his wife to bring out his toga. Then, dressed in his toga, he hurries with the messengers to the senate.

When he approaches the city, the fathers come to meet him and lead him into the senate. There they say, 'You alone can save the city. And so we appoint you dictator. Lead the army against the enemy and save the city from great danger.'

Cincinnatus saves Rome

The next day Cincinnatus leads the army against the enemy. At midnight he draws near the camp of the enemy. Then he orders his soldiers to surround the enemy and raise loud shouts. Both the enemy and the consul's army hear the shouts. The consul says, 'Listen to those shouts, soldiers. The Romans are bringing help and already attacking the enemy. Break out of the camp and attack the enemy yourselves.' So he says, and leads his soldiers into battle.

Now the Romans are attacking the enemy from both sides. They (the enemy) are terrified. They despair and soon surrender. They lay down their arms and depart to their own territory.

Cincinnatus leads the Roman soldiers back to the city. The fathers lead him into the city in triumph. All the citizens rejoice and hold a feast. So Cincinnatus saves the city. But he soon returns home, takes off his toga, and works again in his field.

1 When Cincinnatus approaches the enemy, he orders his men to surround them and raise loud shouts.

2 The besieged consul tells his men to break out of the camp and attack the enemy.

3 The enemy despair because they are being attacked from both sides. They surrender, lay down their arms and retire to their own territory.

4 The senators come out to meet him and lead him into the city in triumph.

5 Cincinnatus takes off his toga, returns to his farm and gets back to work.

6 The moral might be that in a crisis it is not riches and honours that count, but courage and patriotism, which are found even in poor men.

Exercise 15.2

1 Mercury himself orders Aeneas to sail to Italy.
2 He (Aeneas) is unwilling to do this.
3 But he cannot neglect the orders of the gods themselves.
4 He hurries to his comrades and tells them to prepare the ships.
5 On that very day (on that day itself) Dido learns this (these things).
6 She herself summons Aeneas and asks him about this (these things).
7 Aeneas makes this reply to her: 'Jupiter himself orders me to make for Italy.'
8 When the Trojans sail from Libya, Dido herself kills herself with her own hand.

Exercise 15.3

nom.	magnum mare	haec puella
acc.	magnum mare	hanc puellam
gen.	magnī maris	huius puellae
dat.	magnō marī	huic puellae
abl.	magnō marī	hāc puellā

nom.	pater ipse	ingentia saxa
acc.	patrem ipsum	ingentia saxa
gen.	patris ipsīus	ingentium saxōrum
dat.	patrī ipsī	ingentibus saxīs
abl.	patre ipsō	ingentibus saxīs

nom.	marītī trīstēs	illī senēs
acc.	marītōs trīstēs	illōs senēs
gen.	marītōrum trīstium	illōrum senum
dat.	marītīs trīstibus	illīs senibus
abl.	marītīs trīstibus	illīs senibus

Exercise 15.4

1 The enemy are surrounding us; we refuse to stay here; we must break out of the camp.
2 The consul himself is afraid of the enemy and refuses to lead the army against them.
3 No one can save us except Cincinnatus himself. And so summon him to the city.
4 'Cincinnatus, lead this army against the enemy and take help to the consul's legions.'
5 Cincinnatus leads the army against the enemy; he defeats the enemy in battle and saves both the consul himself and his legions.

Exercise 15.5

1 post cēnam Flaccus saepe vult fābulas puerīs nārrāre.
2 Quīntus semper cupit fābulās audīre dē bellīs mīlitibusque.

3 hae fābulae Flaccō ipsī placent, quī eās bene nārrat.
4 Horātia nōn vult haec audīre; et Scintilla et ipsa fābulās audīre cupiunt dē fēminīs Rōmānīs.
5 ubi Flaccus Quīntusque absunt/nōn adsunt, Scintilla nōnnumquam fābulās nārrat dē fēminīs.
6 Horātia hās fābulās laeta audit.

Chapter 16

Cartoon captions

1 Cloelia leads the women to the Tiber and swims across the river.
2 Porsinna is extremely angry; he says to the Romans, 'You are breaking the treaty. Hand over Cloelia to me at once.'
3 The Romans hand Cloelia over to Porsinna, who returns to the camp of the enemy.
4 The Romans commemorate Cloelia's courage by an outstanding honour; for in the Sacred Way they set up a statue of her sitting on horseback.

The courage of Cloelia

The next day while Horatia is sitting in the garden with her mother, she says this: 'Mother dear, Cincinnatus was a brave man and good. Haven't women too shown such great courage?' Scintilla replied, 'Certainly, dear daughter, there were many women who showed the greatest courage, like Cloelia.' Horatia says, 'Tell me, please (if you will) about Cloelia.' Scintilla says, 'Listen, Horatia. I will tell you about the courage of Cloelia.'

Many years ago the Etruscans conquer the Romans in battle but cannot take the city. And so they surround the whole city; they place a garrison on the hill called Janiculum across the Tiber; they guard the river with many ships. The Romans cannot import corn into the city; the citizens are starving but they bravely resist and refuse to surrender on any terms. At length the king of the Etruscans, called Porsinna, himself proposes terms of peace: he is willing to cease from the siege but demands hostages from the Romans. The Romans accept these terms and hand over hostages to Porsinna. The Etruscans lead off their garrison from the Janiculum and pitch camp not far from the Tiber.

Among the hostages are several women. One of these, a maiden called Cloelia, decides to escape from the hands of the enemy. She gives the guards the slip, escapes from the camp, leads a band of women to the Tiber. She swims across the river and leads all the women safe into the city. At first Porsinna is extremely angry and tells the Romans to return all the hostages to him; then he ceases from his anger and, changing to admiration for Cloelia's courage, he says this to the Romans: 'You are breaking the treaty, but if you return Cloelia to me, I shall not only keep her unharmed but I will also free the rest of the women.' The Romans accept these terms and hand over Cloelia, who returns willingly to the camp of the enemy. Porsinna frees the rest of the women. So the peace is renewed.

The Romans commemorate Cloelia's courage with an outstanding honour, for they set up a statue of her at the top of the Sacred Way sitting on horseback.

'The story of Cloelia, Horatia, teaches us this: not only men but women too can show the greatest courage and are worthy of the greatest honour.'

1 She decided to escape from the hands of the enemy.
2 She gave her guards the slip and swam across the Tiber with a group of women.
3 Porsinna demanded that all the hostages should be returned. He changed his mind from anger to admiration for Cloelia's courage and asked that only she should be returned.
4 They set up a statue of her on horseback at the top of the Sacred Way.
5 It proved that women too showed great courage and were worthy of the greatest honour.

Appendix: Ciceronis filius

Cicero is dictating letters to his secretary Tiro. Suddenly someone knocks on the door. In runs a slave. 'Master,' he says, 'I bring you very good news. Terentia has given birth to a little son. Both mother and baby are well.' 'You really do bring me good news,' says Cicero. 'Tiro, tell the slaves to get horses ready. We must hurry to Terentia.'

Soon the horses are ready. Cicero and Tiro at once leave Rome and hurry towards Arpinum. The next day they arrive at the villa. Tullia, Cicero's daughter, who is now ten years old, hears their arrival. She runs to the door and greets her father. 'Come, father,' she says; 'hurry up. The baby is very beautiful.' She leads her father into the reception room. There on a couch lies Terentia, pale but happy; near the couch is a cradle, in which sleeps the tiny baby.

Cicero goes to his wife and gives her a kiss. 'Dear wife,' he says, 'how are you?' He looks at the baby. 'How beautiful the baby is,' he says. 'How glad I am that you are well.' So he says, and lifts the baby from the cradle; he smiles at his little son and says, 'Greetings, little son. Greetings, Marcus. For so I name you.' He hands the baby to a maidservant and sits by

Terentia. For some time he stays with his wife. At length he says, 'You are tired, dearest. You must sleep.' The maidservant carries the baby out of the reception room; four slaves carry Terentia on her couch to the bedroom.

The next day Cicero returns to Rome; for he is standing for the consulship and is occupied with much business. He gives little Marcus a kiss; he says goodbye to his wife and daughter. Then he rides out of the courtyard with Tiro.

While he is little, Marcus usually lives in the villa. His mother and father are often away; for his father is an important man, who, when Marcus is two years old, is made consul. A nurse looks after him, and Tullia, who is very fond of her brother, is usually there. The villa is large enough but not splendid, sited in the Sabine hills. Marcus' father oftens returns there when he is not busy with public affairs; for he always wants to see his son and enjoys visiting his home. Cicero's brother, Quintus Cicero, often comes to the villa with his wife Pomponia and son Quintus. Marcus is happy when Quintus is there; for he likes Quintus and plays with him for ages.

Marcus is in his fifth year when Cicero decides to take him to Rome. There he lives in a magnificent house sited on the Palatine hill. The house is always full of people. Many slaves and maidservants run about performing their duties. Many clients come to the house early in the morning and greet his father. Senators come to his father and ask for his advice. His father is usually busy; he dictates long letters to his secretary; often he has to go to the senate and is away for a long time while the senators discuss public affairs. His mother also is always busy; for she is mistress of the household; she controls all the slaves and all the maidservants; and she often receives noble ladies who come to the house and pay their respects to her.

Marcus is now looked after not by a nurse but by a Greek tutor. He teaches Marcus both Latin and Greek letters; he usually speaks to Marcus in Greek. He (Marcus) does not enjoy his studies; for he always wants to play. But little by little he learns both to speak and to write in Greek.

When summer comes, the whole household goes away from the city into the hills to a country villa; for they cannot bear the heat of summer in the city. There Marcus is on holiday. His cousin Quintus often comes to the villa. The boys play in the fields, visit the farm and catch fish in the river. When autumn comes, they return to the city. Marcus very much enjoys these holidays.

When Marcus is in his seventh year, enemies pass (bring) a law against Cicero. He is very afraid of his enemies and decides to flee into exile. He tells Terentia to leave Rome and stay in a country villa. He sadly departs from Rome and sails to Greece. Terentia takes

the whole household to the villa and stays there while
Cicero is away. Marcus misses his father but is glad
that he is having such a long holiday. Meanwhile
Cicero writes unhappy letters to Terentia and always
longs to return to Rome. The next year his friends pass
(bring) a new law and recall him from exile.

When Cicero returns to Rome, he calls his family
back to the city. While he is away, his house has been
destroyed by his enemies, but Cicero quickly builds a
large and magnificent new house. Marcus is sad
because he has to leave the country but is glad that his
father is there. Now his father himself takes charge of
his studies; Marcus has to study much harder.

A few years later, when Marcus is fourteen years
old, the senators send Cicero to Cilicia to govern the
province. Cicero leaves Rome reluctantly but decides
to take Marcus with him. They must complete a long
and laborious journey. First they sail to Greece and
stay a long time in Athens; Marcus visits all the
monuments and makes new friends amongst Greek
boys.

Then they journey by land. They proceed slowly
and on the way visit the famous cities of Asia. When at
last they reach Cicilia, the province is in great danger,
because enemies are attacking the frontier. Cicero has
to wage war against them. When he (Cicero) meets the
enemy, Marcus wants to watch the battle, but his father
tells him to stay in the camp. Cicero defeats the enemy
and drives them from the province.

The next year Cicero leaves Cilicia and takes
Marcus back home. When they return to Rome, civil
war is threatening the republic. Cicero is extremely
busy and cannot look after his son's studies. And so he
sends Marcus to the school of Orbilius. Marcus is a
reluctant student; he is now a young man and wants to
leave school. But he makes many friends; amongst
others he meets a young man called Quintus Horatius
Flaccus, who has lately arrived from Apulia. He is
modest and witty; Marcus likes him and introduces him
to his father. Cicero is delighted that his son has so
modest and industrious a friend; for Quintus enjoys his
studies and works hard; but Marcus always wants to
play with smart young men and often drinks too much
wine with them.

Attainment test 1   **to be taken after chapter 8 (40 minutes)**

Read the following passage carefully and then answer the questions below:

Scintilla et Horātia ad fontem festīnant. magnās urnās portant. in
viā Quīntum vident; ille lentē ā lūdō redit. mātrem salūtat et
'quid facitis, māter?' inquit; 'cūr festīnātis?' Scintilla respondet,
'festīnāmus quod aquam in casā nōn habēmus; et pater iam ab
5 agrō redit. venī hūc et hanc urnam portā.' sed Quīntus 'ad silvam
festīnō,' inquit; 'omnēs amīcī mē exspectant.' et in silvam currit.
      Scintilla irāta est; 'cūr nōn iuvat nōs Quīntus?' inquit; 'malus
puer est. venī, Horātia; festīnā.' ad fontem adveniunt et aquam
celeriter dūcunt. ad casam lentē redeunt, quod urnae gravēs sunt.
10 Horātia mox fessa est; in terrā sedet, labōre cōnfecta. sed Scintilla Flaccum videt; ille bovēs ab agrō redūcit. Scintilla eum
vocat et 'Flacce,' inquit, 'manē. exspectā nōs. aquam ā fonte
portāmus et valdē fessae sumus.' Flaccus ad eās accurrit et 'ecce!'
inquit, 'adsum. tū, Horātia, urnam trāde et bovēs cūrā.' Horātia
15 laeta urnam trādit et bovēs dūcit. Scintilla et Flaccus urnās
portant et mox omnēs ad casam adsunt.

fontem	spring
urnās	water pots
quod because; **habēmus** we have
hanc this
silvam wood
gravēs heavy
labōre cōnfecta worn out by toil
bovēs oxen
valdē very
trāde hand over

1 Translate the first paragraph.   (30)

2 How does Scintilla feel when Quintus runs off, and why does she feel like this?   (1+2)

3 Why do Scintilla and Horatia come back from the spring more slowly than they
go there? What does Horatia do when she gets tired?   (2+1)

4 At the end of the passage what are (a) Horatia and (b) Flaccus doing?
Why is Horatia now **laeta** (*l.* 15)?   (1+1+1)

5 Give one example each of the following from the second paragraph:
a verb in the 3rd person singular (he, she or it); a verb in the 1st person plural (we);
a verb in the imperative; an adverb.   (4)

6 What case are the following words in and why? Are they singular or plural?
fontem (*l.* 8); **urnās** (*l.* 15); **omnēs** (*l.* 16).   (6)

7 Give an English word derived from **agrō** (*l.* 11).   (1)

TOTAL: (50)

Attainment test 2   **to be taken after chapter II (40 minutes)**

Read the following passage carefully and then answer the questions below:

On his voyage home from Troy, Odysseus (*Ulixēs*) comes to the island of Circe

Ulixēs, dum ab urbe Trōiā domum nāvigat, ad īnsulam venit
ignōtam. comitēs iubet in lītore manēre, sed ipse collem
ascendit. ubi ad summum collem advenit, fūmum videt in
caelum surgentem. ad nāvem redit et aliōs comitum iubet
5 prope nāvem manēre, aliōs in īnsulam mittit; 'in īnsulam
festīnāte,' inquit. 'quis hīc habitat? cognōscere cupiō.'

     illī in īnsulam festīnant et tandem casam in silvā vident.
ubi ad casam accēdunt, multōs lupōs multōsque leōnēs prope
casam vident. valdē timent. mox fēminam audiunt canentem.
10 ubi clāmant, Circē ē iānuā casae exit eōsque in casam vocat.
ūnus sōlus extrā manet, quod perīculum timet; cēterōs Circē
in casam dūcit et 'sedēte,' inquit, 'et cēnāte.'

     sed mala venēna cibō miscet. ubi cibum edunt, statim
suēs fiunt. deinde Circē eōs in stabulum suum pellit iubetque
15 in terrā iacēre.

urbe city	
ignōtam unknown	
ipse he himself; **summum** the top of	
fūmum smoke; **surgentem** rising	
aliōs…aliōs some…others	
cognōscere to find out	
lupōs wolves; **leōnēs** lions	
canentem singing	
extrā outside	
mala venēna poisons	
cibō in the food; **miscet** she mixes	
edunt they eat; **suēs** pigs	
fiunt they become; **deinde** then	
stabulum pigsty; **pellit** she drives	

1 Translate the first paragraph.   (25)

2 What do Odysseus' companions see when they explore the island?
What do they see next? What is their reaction?   (1+2+1)

3 What is Circe doing when they come to her house?
Why does she come out to see them?   (2)

4 One man does not accept Circe's invitation. What does he do and why?   (2)

5 What does Circe do to Odysseus' companions?   (4)

6 What part of what verbs are the following: **exit** (*l.* 10); **sedēte** (*l.* 12), **iacēre** (*l.* 15)?   (3)

7 In what case are the following words, and why: **silvā** (*l.* 7); **multōs** (*l.* 8); **casae** (*l.* 10)?   (6)

8 Give one example each from the second paragraph of: a preposition followed by an
ablative (not **in**); a preposition followed by an accusative; an adverb; an imperative.   (4)

TOTAL: (50)

Attainment test 3 **to be taken after chapter 16 (40 minutes)**

Read the following passage carefully and then answer the questions below:

The hero Hercules and the monster Cacus

prope Tiberis rīpās habitant rēx Evander populusque eius pauper.	**rīpās** banks
in casīs parvīs vīvunt sed contentī omnēs sunt et laetī; ūnum	
sōlum perīculum timent.	
nam spēlunca quaedam est prope flūmen in colle. hīc habitat	**spēlunca** cave
5 mōnstrum ingēns, sēmihomō nōmine Cācus quī flammās ex ōre	**ōre** mouth
spīrat, hominēs rapit et saevē occīdit. sīc populum tōtum diū	**spīrat** breathes; **rapit** seizes
terret. sed tandem advenit hērōs quīdam, nōmine Herculēs, quī	**saevē** savagely
eōs illō terrōre līberat.	**illō terrōre** from that fear
nam ad eum locum Herculēs venit cum taurīs ingentibus	**taurīs** bulls
10 quōs ex Hispāniā ad Graeciam dūcit. Cācus, ubi taurōs videt,	
cōnstituit eōs rapere. itaque, dum Herculēs dormit, in spēluncam	
suam eōs dūcit. postrīdiē, ubi Herculēs ē somnō surgit, taurōs	
vidēre nōn potest. diū trīstis quaerit. tandem mūgītum taurōrum	**mūgītum** the mooing, lowing
audit. summā īrā commōtus, ad spēluncam accēdit collemque	
15 dīripit. magnā vōce clāmat et 'venī hūc, Cāce,' inquit, 'taurōsque	**dīripit** tears open
mihi redde. nōn potes mē fugere. mors tē manet.' Cācus territus	
est et vix resistit. sīc facile vincit eum Herculēs et mōnstrum illud	**facile** easily
horrendum iacet in terrā mortuum.	**horrendum** terrible

1 Where do Evander and his people live? (2)

2 Describe their living conditions. How do the people feel about living there? (2+3)

3 **sēmihomō** (*l.* 5): **sēmi** = half. What do you think Cacus was like? (2)

4 In what two ways is the horrific nature of Cacus conveyed (*ll.* 5–6)? (2)

5 In what case are the following words and why:
perīculum (*l.* 3); **quī** (*l.* 5); **somnō** (*l.* 12); **eum** (*l.* 17)? (8)

6 Give an English word derived from (a) **habitant** (*l.* 1); (b) **populus** (*l.* 1); (c) **spīrat** (*l.* 6) (3)

7 Translate the third paragraph (*ll.* 9–18). (25)

8 What impression do you get of Hercules from this passage? (3)

TOTAL: (50)

Answers to the attainment tests

Attainment test I, to be taken after chapter 8

1   Scintilla and Horatia hurry to the spring. They carry large water pots. On the road they see Quintus; he is coming back slowly from school. He greets his mother and says, 'What are you doing, mother? Why are you hurrying?' Scintilla replies, 'We are hurrying because we do not have water in the house; and father is now coming back from the field. Come here and carry this water pot.' But Quintus says, 'I'm hurrying to the wood; all my friends are waiting for me.' And he runs into the wood (30).

2   She feels angry (1) because Quintus has been a bad boy in not helping them (2).

3   The water pots are now heavy because they are full of water (2). She sits on the ground (1).

4   (a) Horatia is leading the oxen (1) and (b) Flaccus is carrying the water pots (1).
    Horatia is happy because she has got rid of her (heavy) water pot (1).

5   **est/iuvat/inquit/sedet/videt/redūcit/vocat/accurrit/trādit/dūcit** (1); **portāmus/sumus** (1);
    venī/festīnā/manē/exspectā/trāde/cūrā (1); **lentē/celeriter/mox/valdē** (1).

6   accusative, after **ad**, singular (2); accusative, object of verb, plural (2);
    nominative, subject of verb, plural (2).

7   agriculture/agricultural (1).

Attainment test 2, to be taken after chapter II

1   While Odysseus sails home from the city of Troy, he comes to an unknown island. He orders his companions to stay on the shore, but he climbs a hill. When he reaches the top of the hill, he sees smoke rising into the sky. He goes back to the ship and orders some of his companions to stay near the ship and sends others into the island. 'Hurry into the island,' he says. 'Who lives here? I want to know' (25).

2   a house (1); many wolves and (many) lions (2); they are very afraid (1).

3   singing (1); they shout (1).

4   He stays outside (1) because he is frightened (of the danger) (1).

5   She gives them food mixed with poison (1); they become pigs (1);
    she drives them into her pigsty (1); and orders them to lie on the ground (1).

6   third person singular of **exeō** (1); plural imperative of **sedeō** (1); present infinitive of **iaceō** (1).

7   ablative, after **in** (2); accusative, adjective agreeing with **lupōs** (or **leōnēs**) (2);
    genitive, of the house (2).

8   **ē** (*l.* 10) (1); **in** (*ll.* 7, 10, 12)/**ad** (*l.* 8)/**prope** (*l.* 8) (1); **tandem** (*l.* 7)/**valdē** (*l.* 9)/**mox** (*l.* 9) (1);
    sedēte (*l.* 12)/**cēnāte** (*l.* 12) (1).

Attainment test 3, to be taken after chapter 16

1   They live near the banks of the Tiber (2).

2   They are poor and they live in small houses (2).
They are content and happy (2), but frightened of one thing (1).

3   a subjective answer: brutal, huge, monstrous, animalistic – these are possibilities,
but other suggestions may well qualify for marks (2).

4   He breathes flames (from his mouth) (1) and (seizes and savagely) kills men (1).

5   accusative, object of verb (2); nominative, subject of verb(s) (2);
ablative, after ē (2); accusative, object of verb (2).

6   (a) inhabit/inhabitant/habitation/habitat (1);
(b) population/populate/populace/popular (1);
(c) inspire/inspiration/respiration, etc. (1).

7   For Hercules comes to that place with the huge bulls which he is leading from Spain (Hispania) to
Greece (Graecia). When Cacus sees the bulls, he decides to seize them. And so, while Hercules is
sleeping, he leads them into his cave. The next day, when Hercules rises from sleep, he cannot see
the bulls. He searches sadly for a long time. At length he hears the mooing of the bulls. Moved with
the greatest anger, he goes to the cave and tears open the hill. He shouts with a great voice and says,
'Come here, Cacus, and give me back my bulls. You cannot escape me. Death awaits you.' Cacus is
terrified and scarcely resists. Thus Hercules easily conquers him and that terrible monster lies on the
ground dead (25).

8   a subjective answer: heroic, passionate, violent, a man of action, fiercely protective of his property,
a civilizing force – these are possibilities, but other suggestions may well qualify for marks (3).